You Goddess!

also by E. Foley & B. Coates

What Would Boudicca Do?
Homework for Grown-ups
Advanced Homework for Grown-ups
Homework for Grown-ups Quiz Book
Shakespeare for Grown-ups

You Goddess!

Lessons in Being Legendary from Awesome Immortals

E. FOLEY & B. COATES

illustrated by

GEORGIA PERRY

faber

First published in 2020
by Faber & Faber Limited
Bloomsbury House
74–77 Great Russell Street
London WC1B 3DA

Typeset by Faber & Faber Limited
Printed in the UK by CPI Group (UK) Ltd, Croydon CR0 4YY

A CIP record for this book
is available from the British Library

ISBN 978-0-571-35996-7

MIX
Paper from responsible sources
FSC® C020471
FSC www.fsc.org

2 4 6 8 10 9 7 5 3 1

To Laura, as wise as Athena,
as ambitious as Inanna,
as laughter-bringing as Uzume

Like breath or a balloon, I'm rising,
I hover six inches in the air
in my blazing swan-egg of light.
You think I'm not a goddess?
Try me.
This is a torch song.
Touch me and you'll burn.

'Helen of Troy Does Countertop Dancing'
Margaret Atwood

Contents

Introduction

What springs to mind when you think of the word 'goddess'? Divine feminine energy? Mother Earth? Ancient Greek ladies wafting around in white dresses causing mischief? Hollywood stars? 'Domestic goddesses' or 'sex goddesses'? Or even Anastasia Steele's exuberant 'inner goddess' who spends a lot of *Fifty Shades of Grey* salsa-ing and pole-vaulting in excitement about her romantic escapades? (Each to her own.)

There are two definitions of the term 'goddess' in the dictionary – 1. a female deity, or 2. a woman who is powerfully attractive and beautiful. Wrapped up in the broader associations of the word are lots of attributes that sound super-fun and enjoyable (Beauty! Allure! Meddling!), alongside more tricky inferences about what our culture assumes to be the ultimate qualities a woman can possess (Beauty! Allure! Meddling!).

The goddesses' stories in this book reflect the expectations that both hamper women *and* provide us with timeless models of how to live our best lives.

You'll find empowering examples of female excellence in these pages, including deities from every corner of the globe – we travel from Ancient Greece to Japan, from Scandinavia to the Americas, from Polynesia to the Middle East – to help inject a little mythical magnificence into your day.

As long as there have been humans, there have been myths. We've always used stories peopled with magical beings and extraordinary acts of bravery or epic failure to help us better understand our role in a universe that is often frightening and illogical. Our ancient ancestors were facing a more brutal existence than we are when they developed the religions that sustained them, but despite all of the comforts at our disposal and all the scientific breakthroughs that have replaced the legends that used to explain our environment, we still struggle with finding our place in the world. And the big questions remain: who am I? What am I doing here? How can I be a good person? Why am I so addicted to my phone? Can you wear boots with midi skirts? How do I do contouring?

Millions of people find the answers to (some of) these questions in their faith, holding these tenets as truth, while regarding stories from other religions as myths. The word 'myth' carries an implication of fiction or falsity. As the celebrated poet and controversial scholar of mythology Robert Graves said, 'Mythology is the study of whatever religious or heroic legends are so foreign to a student's experience that he cannot believe them to be true.'

Goddesses appear in many religions that have huge numbers of active adherents today, such as Hinduism and Shinto, as well as many that are no longer commonly followed, such as Graeco-Roman and Celtic. The largest faiths active in the world today focus on central male gods, although with significant female figures. The only current Western religion that worships a pre-eminent goddess is Wicca.

In this book we take a broad definition of what makes a goddess and make no judgement about whether a goddess's feats are true or not; we seek to approach all their stories from a respectfully secular point of view. Many of the stories we recount here are precious and sacred to specific communities. We have aimed to write with courtesy and attention, conscious that our position as outsiders to many of the cultures covered in this book is particularly uncomfortable given the history of conquest, exploitation and cultural high-handedness and appropriation that white Europeans have been guilty of throughout history. We are aware that it is difficult for us to escape our own cultural baggage when approaching these subjects, or to fully understand them in the way their initiated believers do. We approached all the lore in this book with an open curiosity and it's been a privilege to learn about mythologies that weren't well known to us before we began our investigations. Our eyes were opened to many stories and ideas that we hadn't encountered before. There are multifarious myths that deal with goddesses beyond the Graeco-Roman ones many of us are taught about in school; we hope *You Goddess!* introduces you to some new deities and inspires you to find out more about the histories, cultures or religions they spring from. The joy of writing this book has been the learning experience it has given us, but we are aware that learning is never finished.

Across the globe, when you reach back into ancient history real women generally don't get much of a look-in. Despite the hopeful efforts of twentieth-century feminist archaeologists, it turns out there probably wasn't a golden time or place in pre-history where politics was run by women.* It's always been a man's world. Thanks to the pervasiveness of the patriarchy,

* The archaeological discovery of many statues of lovely booby female figurines like the 30,000-year-old Venus of Willendorf led people to believe that there was widespread worship of a mother goddess in pre-historic times, and that perhaps this also meant that society was run by females. Sadly this theory has been rejected by most modern analysts, who don't feel the available evidence supports it.

most myths concern themselves with the heroic deeds of men. But, across cultures, the one arena in which women have been respected and allowed to take their place next to male counterparts doing equal jobs for (sometimes) equal reward has been the celestial realm of folklore and myth. Admittedly, to qualify for this unique position they had to be superhuman, but we can still learn something from the high standards deity demands.

We've looked to each goddess in this book to help illuminate an attribute that we can cultivate, or a subject we can explore, to help us with our own personal success, mental health and confidence today. We've thought about the anxieties that come up again and again for many twenty-first-century women and found the immortals who can teach us most about putting them in their place. We won't be doing this by chanting or garlanding our hair or dancing barefoot in the midnight dew (although all of that sounds great). We'll be doing it by learning about their extravagant exploits, their challenges, their superpowers and the way their stories have changed over time. We'll investigate how to confront our fears, establish our independence, manage our reputations, embrace our bodies, support other women, say no, prioritise self-care and make our own luck, as well as much, much more.

The stories that have come down to us were once mostly the realm of wandering male poets, scribes or authors. As twenty-first-century female readers we see these fables through a specific lens. To an eleventh-century audience the story of the Welsh flower maiden Blodeuwedd warned against women's inherent sluttiness but to us it reads as a go-getting tale of female emancipation. Our other goddesses' stories are also often ripe for reinterpretation and the lessons we learn from them might sometimes be unexpected. The ways in which our heavenly sisters have been reinvented over the centuries tell us a lot about changing standards of femininity and womanhood. There are often different versions of each goddess's myth so we have picked the most well known or enlightening from our point of view. We've looked at these accounts from the perspective of modern women finding surprising points of connection with our sisters through the ages and across continents. If you'd like to explore more expert opinions and academic investigations into some of the themes that come up in this book you can find a list of sources at the back.

The goddesses here allow us to interrogate female stereotypes* that have endured from ancient times to

* If you tend to get your types in a muddle: a stereotype is a widely held but oversimplified image of a particular type of person; an

today: we'll look at the Amazon or 'strong woman', the nurturing selfless mother, the wise or wicked hag, the overweening bitch, the temptress, the innocent damsel in distress and the manic pixie dream girl. Our media still constantly asks questions about what women can achieve: can women be funny? Can they be leaders? Can they succeed in tech? Is it OK for them to be promiscuous? Is it OK if they don't want children? What if they want children *and* a career? WTF! How can that work? Can they get old and still be attractive and useful? Can't they just *relax*?

After all, there is another side to being a goddess, along with all the glamour and glory: powerful women are dangerous. They are unnerving enough that in many myths they are the deities in charge of death and destruction. You only have to look at Kali* or Hel** or Tiamat*** to get the clear message that goddesses can be scary AF. We'll see what we can learn

archetype is a universally understood symbol which recurs in culture; a haplotype is a set of alleles of different genes that are closely linked on one chromosome, and has nothing to do with this book.

* Hindu goddess of death and time, usually depicted with four arms holding a sword, trident, severed head and a tidy bowl to catch the blood (domestic goddess points). You'll find more about her on pp. 112–18.

** Norse goddess of the underworld. Stylishly embodied, with on-point smoky eyeshadow, by Cate Blanchett in *Thor: Ragnarok*.

*** Babylonian goddess of the sea and chaos, often depicted as a fierce dragon, as in the cult 1980s TV show *Dungeons and Dragons*.

from this as well as from the more positive aspects our goddesses have to share. Whether you dip into *You Goddess!* for individual titbits or read it all the way through from start to finish, we hope you'll find that it is about celebrating female power in all its forms. It is a superheroine superboost which we hope you'll want to share with your girlfriends, sisters, mothers and daughters – with every goddess in your life.

You Goddess!

Athena
and Being a 'Strong' Woman

CLASSICAL, GREECE

ALSO KNOWN AS

Grey-Eyed Athena,
Pallas, The Unwearying,
Minerva (in Ancient Rome)

SKILLS

Intelligence, Creativity, Strategy,
Being a Man's Woman

RESPONSIBILITIES

War, Wisdom, Tech, Crafts, Politics,
Philosophy, Owls

Athena is one of the best-known goddesses in the Western world. She is a member of the famously hectic Olympian family of deities who were worshipped as far back as the second millennium BCE in Ancient Greece. The Olympians engaged in all kinds of heroic and terrible acts, usually to the ultimate detriment of the mortal humans they treated as pets. Athena was born in an unusual manner, which set the pattern for her life. Her father, king of the gods Zeus, impregnated and then swallowed her mother, Metis, after tricking her into turning into a fly. He took this rather drastic action because of a prophecy that Metis' children might end up more powerful than him. (Even gods are scared of prophecies.) Athena gestated inside Zeus and eventually caused him such a massive headache that, instead of popping a paracetamol, he got another god to cut open his head with an axe. An unusual newborn, Athena jumped out fully grown and dressed in armour.

From this point on the stories told about Athena, obviously written predominantly by men,* focused on the fact that she was born from her father, that she was

* The long history of the exclusion of the majority of women from education has only recently ended. In Britain 180 years ago, 60 per cent of women were still illiterate. (The current global adult literacy rate is 90 per cent for men and 83 per cent for women.)

good at manly stuff like fighting and thinking, and that she frequently undermined the sisterhood by favouring male heroes like Orestes (whom she let off a matricide charge) and punishing women who got on her nerves. A famous example of the latter was Arachne, a woman who matched her at the top female sport of competitive weaving. Athena turned Arachne into a spider as punishment for her uppity cheek. There was also poor Medusa, whom she turned into a snake-headed monster because she had the audacity to get raped in Athena's temple. One of the quotes invented for this daunting goddess by the playwright Sophocles is: 'To laugh at your enemies – what sweeter laughter can there be than that?'

Despite this, Athena has always been highly regarded because she was undoubtedly powerful and influential over the affairs of men, at a time when mortal women had no such glory. She is the goddess of war, alongside her brother Ares (who is more accurately the god of mindless violence and pub brawls), and the goddess of technology and crafts like shipbuilding and metalwork. (If she were around today she'd probably excel at coding and engineering, like Shuri from *Black Panther*.) Her famed intelligence and political nous were also considered masculine qualities; her origin story implies that wisdom and invention quite literally spring from the brains of men. This meant that clever heroes like Odysseus respected her intellect and advice, rather than just respecting her godliness, as they might have done with her sexy cousin Aphrodite, the goddess of love (see pp. 79–88).

Athena's determination to keep herself firmly on the shelf in a state of permanent virginity, as well as her macho outfit and talents, allowed her to be mates with the lads. Some scholars see this absence of sexuality as a crucial element of her association with ingenuity: non-virgin women were supposed to find their creativity in sex, childbearing and playing endless games of peekaboo with their babies. Athena sidestepped this to focus on her craft and tech hobbies.

As guardian of Athens, which was the historic centre of democracy, Athena is still regarded as a symbol of political freedom and justice. She won her ownership of the city that now bears her name in a gift-giving competition with the sea god, her uncle Poseidon. In order to impress the citizens of the town, Poseidon banged his famous trident onto the ground and produced a spring, which unfortunately was salty and so not much use to them. When Athena slammed down her spear an olive tree sprouted, which was far preferred for providing food, oil and wood (she also invented other handy things like rakes, numbers and trumpets). There is still a protected olive tree growing on top of the Acropolis in Athens inside the ruins of a temple dedicated to both Poseidon and Athena. Athena's most common sidekick is an owl but she is also depicted with snakes: one legend tells of a serpent who used to guard the Acropolis on her behalf, and she has Medusa's snake hairdo* prominently displayed on her *aegis*, or shield.

The Romans loved incorporating Greek religion into their own. Athena's Roman incarnation, Minerva, was less fighty and more intellectual than her Greek counterpart. The great Latin poet Ovid noted what an excellent multitasker she was, calling her 'the goddess of a thousand works'.** She was certainly a flexible goddess: as the Roman Empire spread through Europe in the first century BCE she was sometimes mixed up with similar local goddesses, like the Gaulish Belisama in the south of France and the British healing goddess Sulis. You can still visit the temple of Sulis-Minerva in Bath.

* The image of Medusa's head is called the gorgoneion and you'll find it on all those Versace clothes in your wardrobe. Freud thought Medusa's decapitated head was a symbol that represented fears of castration inspired by the terrifying sight of women's genitals (with the snakes representing pubic hair). Possibly not the vibe Versace were after.

** Next time you're busy doing the laundry you can feel a bit grander knowing that you are acting under Athena's aegis: 'Worship her, thou who dost remove stains from damaged garments!' says Ovid.

There's a great deal to admire about a goddess who brings wisdom, can stand up for herself and looks after owls, but Athena is also an example of the patriarchal idea of a 'strong woman', which, while it *sounds* like a compliment, is often a complicated designation. When we talk positively about 'strong female characters' in films, books and telly, what most of us mean is 'a female character who is just as significant and nuanced as any male character'. (We don't really talk about 'strong male characters' because that's considered the norm.) However, 'strong' heroines in the media and popular culture often turn out to be women who are *literally* strong and act quite a lot like men, but in heels. (In films they also inevitably need to spend a bit of time lounging about in luxury underwear at the end of the day after punching all the bad guys. Hi, *Atomic Blonde*!) Through their celebration as exceptional, these 'kick-ass' ladies cast the shadow of 'weakness' over all ordinary women. These kinds of 'strong' women tend not to be frilly or cuddly or cry as much as other women – but why should masculine attributes be the only definition of strength?

'Strong' women are able to put up with shit without complaining – but maybe in truth there *are* things women should be complaining about in order to make the world a better place. Athena is the perfect goddess to look to when questioning these sorts of judgements made on her sex. Her boldness and upper-body strength are certainly impressive when she calls alpha male Ares a 'two-faced liar' and knocks him down with a rock in Homer's *Iliad*, but her most famous stories involve her brain power. When working with the buff heroes she favours, Athena doesn't always appear in her usual warrior-princess outfit; sometimes she is a vulnerable old lady or a little girl.

Disguised as a grandma, she shows both intelligence and fashion sense when she helps Heracles make a snazzy coat out of the Nemean lion by advising him to use the monster's might against it: only the lion's own claws can cut through its hide. She also comes up with the idea of the Trojan Horse, which wins the Trojan War for the Greeks after they use it to sneak inside Troy's walls. Even without her martial artistry, we can look at her through modern eyes and see the positives in a smart female who isn't defined by her sexual attractiveness* and who – without subscribing to the view that it is her very traditional masculinity which makes her great – can beat men at their own game.

* The Trojan warrior, and *Greece's Next Top Goddess* judge, Paris famously judged Aphrodite to be better-looking than Athena.

Freyja
and Breaking the Rules

NORSE, SCANDINAVIA

ALSO KNOWN AS

The Lady, Strife-Stirrer, Vanadis

SKILLS

Seduction, Invisibility,
Magic, Hedonism

RESPONSIBILITIES

Sex, Fertility, Gold, Death,
War, Travel

It can be hard to forge your own way. It's so much easier to run with the crowd, even when you feel like you're not quite on the right path. Your parents, partner and friends can all have forceful ideas about what you should be doing with your life – or what you're doing wrong with it – and it takes a great deal of self-belief and determination to choose a different direction. If you're feeling the need to take a stand against convention, then the Norse warrior goddess Freyja can provide a bit of inspiration.

In the Norse mythology of the Vikings the gods were broadly divided into two groups – the conflict-hungry Aesir, who loved a bit of war and wealth, and the more primal and wild Vanir, who were associated with sex and fertility. These two tribes waged a brutal battle against each other

(over gold, natch) that eventually became so mutually destructive they agreed to swap hostages and form a peace of sorts. So Freyja, the beautiful, mysterious and powerful daughter of the chief Vanir, ended up in Asgard with the likes of father god Odin, hammer-loving Thor and his frenemy foster-uncle, the trickster Loki.

Freyja has the whole treasure chest going on; as a goddess associated with travel she channels the powerful forces of nature: she drives a chariot pulled by cats, rides a boar with golden bristles and has possession of a magical shape-shifting cloak made of falcon feathers. And she, along with Odin, is a master of a form of Norse magic called *seidr*, which is so powerful it can change the course of fate and destiny.

According to the thirteenth-century collection of Old Norse poems known as the *Poetic Edda*, death on the battlefield was the ideal way to go for Norsemen. It guaranteed entrance to Valhalla, Odin's majestic hall where warriors could fight all day and feast every night on an endless supply of wild boar. Lesser known is the fact that Freyja got the pick of the dead – as boss of the Valkyries* she claimed half of all slain warriors.

* Valkyries were excellent flying battle goddesses who descended from the heavens to the battlefield to select which souls would go with Odin to engage in constant fighty training in preparation for Ragnarok (the end of days), and which would head for Freyja's less pugnacious palace.

She was allowed to choose first, and she took them back to her place, a chilled-out meadow called Folkvangr – the meadow of the people. Though later depictions of Freyja in Christian poetry and art cast her as a rather dreamy, floaty, sensual goddess of fertility, it's worth remembering she was right up there with the big guns – worshipped in her own right as a mighty and powerful goddess who did things in her own inimitable way. Many of the Norse gods fell in love with Freyja, giants kept getting up to mischief to grab her attention, mortals worshipped her to encourage bumper crops, and she had the best accessories – of which more later. The stories that swirl around her show a goddess truly in touch with her sexuality and love of the finer things in life.

One famous story involves Freyja's pursuit of the amber necklace Brisingamen – a thing of such blazing beauty and perfection that as soon as she clapped eyes on it she was determined it would be hers. Freyja asked the four dwarves who had created it how much it was worth – she'd pay whatever they wanted. One night with each of them was the answer, and Freyja, being a lady who knew very well her heart's own desire, and entirely unbound by sexual constraint, agreed. Loki, witnessing this, told Odin what she'd done. (Loki liked to go round spilling the tea that she'd slept with all the gods and elves.) Odin saw an opportunity to wield a bit of authority over Freyja. He ordered Loki to steal Brisingamen, which he did by disguising himself as a fly to get into her bedroom. Odin agreed to return the bling to Freyja, on the condition that she would cast a spell to set two kings in perpetual war against each other. (Like the Olympians, Norse gods and goddesses seemed to have a lot of fun toying with the fates of their mortal subjects and often pitted people against each other for a laugh.) Freyja duly set about her task – she *really* wanted that necklace. Her connection with gold was so strong that people used to refer to it as 'Freyja's tears'.

In another story an enemy giant named Thrymm took Thor's hammer hostage (definitely not a symbolic castration, oh no) in order to demand Freyja's hand in marriage. Resisting the classic damsel-in-distress trope, Freyja point blank refused his proposal and in fact came up with a brilliant Plan B to get the hammer back, which beautifully undercut Thor's marauding masculinity: how about, she suggested, Thor indulge in a bit of cross-dressing and disguise himself as the blushing bride instead? She'd even lend him her favourite necklace to help with his look. (Thor pulled off the scam, killing the giant and retrieving his hammer at their wedding dinner. Think of the shock he must've caused the giant aunties.)

We salute Freyja for her unwillingness to blindly follow the orders of her adopted Aesir, and for the pleasure she takes in forging her own path to get just what she wants. It's not a crime to break the rules sometimes, and sometimes it's even *necessary* for us to play fast and loose with convention in order to smash the barriers holding us back from fulfilling our own potential.* Women have spent millennia being told what's right and what's wrong for them, so it's no surprise that we're guilty of being sheep at times. OK, you may not possess a chariot pulled by cats, but there's a lot of fun to be had in travelling your very own road.

* It's fitting that the day on which we get to break free from school or work each week is Freyja's day – we get the word 'Friday' from her name. TFI Freyja's day!

Uzume
and Laughing at Yourself

SHINTO, JAPAN

ALSO KNOWN AS

The Great Persuader, Heaven's Forthright Female, The Heavenly Alarming Female

SKILLS

Dance, Striptease, Stand-Up Comedy

RESPONSIBILITIES

Happiness, Dawn, Marriage, Harmony

The Japanese Shinto goddess Ame-no-Uzume-no-Mikoto is a breath of fresh air. We should all wake up to the brilliance of this dawn deity and embrace her exhilaratingly earthy and playful attitude. Uzume's special talent is to turn a bad situation into something positive, using the power of her sense of humour. A gift for comedy is often underappreciated or considered less important than more serious attributes, but sharing humour can bind people together and definitely makes life more enjoyable. Laughter has been found by scientists to boost your immune system, lower your stress levels, and even protect against heart disease. So perhaps we should all be making more effort to open ourselves up to the lighter side of life. Next time you're feeling a little touchy or low-spirited, turn to Uzume.

Shinto is unusual in the panoply of world religions for having a goddess, Amaterasu, as the central deity, or *kami*. Alongside her there are many other *kami*, some of whom, like Uzume, are personified and some of whom are more like spirits who inhabit or look after places, qualities or natural elements. Uzume is the *kami* of both the dawn and happiness and she is renowned for her gleeful boldness. Her associations with these phenomena are explained in the stories about her in the eighth-century CE books, the *Kojiki** and *Nihon Shoki*.

Amaterasu, the sun goddess, is the ruler of the *kami* and also the ancestor of the Japanese emperor's family. She is represented by the sun disc on the Japanese national flag. Amaterasu's brother Tsukuyomi is god of the moon, in a twist on the more familiar dynamic in which the flashier, golden sun is male and the shy, retiring moon is female. The black sheep of their family is her bad-boy other brother, the storm god Susanoo. Like many of us mere mortals, Susanoo and Amaterasu had a volatile sibling relationship. During one row Susanoo behaved so badly (throwing a flayed divine horse at her) that Amaterasu decided she'd had enough and sealed herself up in a cave.

Because Amaterasu was the sun, her exit had the unfortunate effect of plunging the world into total darkness. Everyone knows how crucial sunlight is to life on earth, and along with a terminal terrestrial outlook, the dark also encouraged murky evil spirits to run riot, so the other *kami* set to work trying to persuade her to give up her subterranean alone time. This proved

* The *Kojiki* is unusually gynotastic as this collection of stories was compiled under the orders of the eighth-century Empress Genmei from the tales memorised by a courtier known as Hiyeda no Are, who is thought by some to be a female descendant of Uzume herself.

tricky until clever Uzume tried something unexpected.

Setting herself up a makeshift stage of an upturned tub, Uzume threw together a theatrical outfit (including a moss belt and leaf headdress) and cracked out a high-energy dance number, during which she flashed her bits and boobs at the other *kami* to make them laugh. Who among us can hear the sound of other people laughing without feeling a burning desire to get in on the joke? Amaterasu couldn't resist investigating the *kami*'s roars of hilarity and stepped out of her cave retreat to see what was going on. Once outside, she was distracted by her own blazingly beautiful reflection in a mirror Uzume had hung up on a branch, and the other *kami* sealed up the cave entrance behind her.

Amaterasu found Uzume's moves so enjoyable that she agreed to stay with her *kami* pals and light up the world again. Uzume became goddess of the dawn because she brought the sun out of darkness. She's clearly the goddess of happiness and laughter because she turned a frightening situation into something warm and convivial by casting aside her own vanity and having an infectiously good time. Uzume's story is closely mirrored by the Greek myth of Baubo and Demeter, where Baubo, the old-lady goddess of fun, cheered up the harvest goddess Demeter, who was fretting about her daughter Persephone being kidnapped by the god of the underworld. Baubo also did a bit of flashing to make Demeter giggle. Humour is, of course, subjective and closely tied to the mores of time and place (as anyone who has read an Ancient Greek 'comedy' will be aware). We spend most of our time laughing at our female friends, but even we find Uzume's set a bit baffling – it was more of a 'you had to be there' kind of gag – but her contemporary audience found it hilarious.

There's a tedious discussion that rears its head periodically in the media about whether women are as funny as men – their lack of visibility on comedy panel shows, in writers' rooms and, in past times, in stand-up is cited as proof that girls just can't raise the chuckles. If you look at online chat about this subject there are an awful lot of helpful blokes making it clear they don't find jokes about periods funny, so who knows what they would have thought of Uzume flashing her lady garden? White, cis, heterosexual men have had the dominant voice in our society for centuries so there's often a lot of noise from them when something isn't purposefully designed to please them.

The 'men are just funnier' line is often explained by evolutionary theories that male animals tend to have to put on a show to attract mates whereas females just sit around judging them and not, therefore, honing any witty badinage or fancy feather displays themselves. However, recent scientific studies suggest that this gendered view of humour is more of a self-fulfilling stereotype than an objective truth. People in our society simply expect men to be funnier and women making jokes are judged more harshly than men (recent research shows that colleagues are more likely to define women's jokes as 'disruptive' where men's are considered helpful). Humour is often associated with extroverts and can even be combative, which connects it to high-status individuals, so Uzume's self-confidence worked in her favour; she was, after all, also known as the Heavenly Alarming Female.

The 'unfunny lady' image is one of many negative female stereotypes; it's connected to both the trouble women have being taken seriously in the first place and a cultural anxiety over women making displays of themselves (isn't it better for everyone if they're at home quietly knitting instead of out there flaunting themselves?). Unsurprisingly, given the focus women's bodies have always received, scholars have been particularly interested in the striptease elements of Uzume's cabaret. The common interpretation of why her nakedness is important in this myth connects the generative and fertile powers of the sun with the same powers in the female body. Uzume got away with behaving in this attention-seeking, immodest way because she was acting, on a metaphorical level, for the good of the universe.

Uzume's dance is said to be the basis of the less risqué sacred *kagura* dancing, which is still performed today, and the mirror which she used to distract Amaterasu is kept in a shrine in the coastal town of Ise. It is part of the sacred regalia of the Japanese emperor and was a key part of the coronation ceremony of Emperor Naruhito in 2019. It was originally brought down to earth by Amaterasu's grandson, Ninigi, who ultimately founded the imperial family when his great-grandson, the first Emperor Jimmu, took power in 660 BCE. Uzume also played a role in this adventure.

When Ninigi was about to step down from heaven to take control of the human realm, his solar grandma noticed that a rather weird and terrifying-looking *kami* was waiting at the border between the two worlds. She sent her trusted conflict-resolution agent, Uzume, to check things out. Uzume approached the *kami*, Sarutahiko, with her trademark jolly attitude and discovered he was actually friendly, despite his ill-favoured appearance. In some accounts they later married. This story explains where Uzume's reputation for bravery comes from.

Her excellent epithet of Heavenly Alarming Female may also link to another story in which she set about menacing marine echinoderms. When Ninigi came to earth, Uzume was in charge of getting all the fish to agree to worship him. Sadly the sea cucumber let the side down as it didn't have a mouth to swear allegiance with. Uzume grabbed a knife and helpfully cut it one so it didn't feel left out.*

Uzume's ability to make fun of herself is connected with her bravery: often the thing we fear most in everyday life is embarrassing ourselves. Again and again people cite fear of humiliation as the strongest force holding them back from following their dreams or stepping outside their comfort zones. If we can embrace the joy of laughing at ourselves, like Uzume, we neutralise shame and get to enjoy the sunshine of a happy and fulfilled life.

* Uzume's funny–scary mixture reminds us of the gorgeously named Inuit goddess Irdlirvirisissong, who is the cousin of the moon god and a bit of a joker. She also loves a bit of comedy dancing but if laughed at she is inclined to freeze humans' intestines and eat them as a sort of tasty ice-cream snack.

Oshun
and Getting What You're Owed

YORUBA, WEST AFRICA

ALSO KNOWN AS

Osun, Oxum, Ochun, Our Lady of Charity, Mamae, The Pre-Eminent Hair-Plaiter with the Coral-Beaded Comb, Goddess of the Sweet Waters

SKILLS

Medicine, Communication, Creativity

RESPONSIBILITIES

Spiritual Balance, Pleasure, Water, Fertility, Love, Money

Stylish, financially astute and an excellent communicator. This reads like a pretty great dating profile, but the goddess Oshun isn't particularly interested in who might want to couple up with her. She is worth more than enough by herself: most of her prize achievements occur when she's acting independently of the other gods in her group. Oshun is not about to go unrewarded for her efforts and she makes no bones about wanting to have a good time and enjoy life to the full. This is what you get if you're the goddess of wealth and pleasure as well as creativity and healing. Happily for Oshun she is one of the most popular goddesses still worshipped today and the offerings left at her shrines are top of the range in every way, gold, perfume, champagne, delicious treats and honey being some of her favourite things.

Oshun is best known as a Yoruba deity, or *orisha*. The religion and culture of the Yoruba people of western Africa have had a huge influence on the world. Through the transportation of slaves to the Americas during the hundreds of years of the abhorrent Atlantic slave trade and other subsequent migrations, Yoruba beliefs have embedded and developed in many other countries, and have influenced local religions such as Cuban Regla de Ocha (also called Santería) and Brazilian Candomblé. The Yoruba concept of a

community of spirits and deities called *orishas* is linked to the belief systems of other African peoples in countries such as Ghana, Benin and Togo. The hundreds of *orishas* in the Yoruba pantheon are an A-list mixture of gods and goddesses, spirits of nature, and past heroes and rulers. In the related Afro-Caribbean religions they are also often combined with Christian saints. Oshun is a woman of such diverse and rich attributes that she is identified with both the Virgin Mary and the Greek goddess Aphrodite (see pp. 79–88), two ladies with contrasting hobbies who generally hang with very different crowds.

Oshun is one of the most significant of all the *orishas.* One pleasing myth points to how central she was during the creation of humanity. Olodumare, the chief creator god, originally sent seventeen *orishas* to earth to fill it with life. All of them apart from Oshun were male and they effectively left her outside the boardroom to order their lunches while they attempted their big, manly, creative endeavour. They failed. Finally, they asked Oshun to help them, and suddenly life bloomed. The long-standing interpretation of this story is that it's very difficult to achieve anything meaningful without women's involvement.

In many portrayals, Oshun is fabulously gorgeous and she takes pity on outcasts, sick children, underdogs and those who are struggling to conceive. In several stories her persuasive power and strategy of using her honeyed sweetness to get what she wants are highlighted. However, the tales also tell us, she doesn't suffer fools, she can be vain, her power can flow in destructive directions, and she has a sinister laugh. She is the boss of fresh fertile waters and their healing potential, but is also responsible for floods and droughts when displeased. Like many potent goddesses she is associated with witchcraft; her love of honey means she's sometimes even said to punish people with Type 2 diabetes.

Oshun's connection with water means she occasionally appears as a mermaid, but whatever form she takes she is always shown as beautifully dressed, usually in yellow, and adorned with gold and brass bracelets, beads, mirrors and fans. Beyoncé channels Oshun in her 'Hold Up' video where you see her bursting through a set of doors on a wave of water, dressed in a dreamy bright yellow dress. (She also makes reference to Oshun's relation, the Yoruba water goddess Yemoja, in her video for 'Spirit'. Yemoja is often depicted as a mermaid dressed in blue.*) It's likely Oshun

* Another mermaid goddess from West Africa who has similar interests to Oshun and Yemoja is Mami Wata. So much for all those who objected to the casting of a black actress as Disney's new Little Mermaid on the grounds that there were no black mermaids: Yemoja and Mami Wata have been around for centuries.

would approve of this homage: she loves a bit of dazzle, and the belief that she can bestow money and fame on her favourites also helps with her influencer status. But despite this focus on her beauty, one story shows her sacrificing her glam looks for the greater good. When the other *orishas* rebelled against Olodumare, resulting in a devastating drought, Oshun took the form of a peacock and flew up to heaven to beg for forgiveness, which she gained. Her beautiful feathers were scorched by the sun on the way and Olodumare sent her back to earth as his messenger, now in the form of a vulture.

Oshun is a complex, multi-layered character, but one who is decidedly effective at whatever she puts her mind to. She is a particularly joyful goddess as she represents making the most of the good things life has to offer. As the goddess of pleasure she enjoys romantic relationships. Her significant beaus are Shango, the god of thunder, and Orunmila, the god of divination, who taught her how to give insight into people's problems and questions using rituals involving casting shells. She has also been adopted as a protector of gay, lesbian, bisexual and transgender people as she represents love in all its forms.

In Nigeria, Oshun is celebrated every August in the Osun-Osogbo festival. This festival takes place in a sacred grove, which is now a UNESCO world heritage site, where she is said to have appeared to the founding inhabitants of the town of Osogbo, next to the river Osun which bears her name. She allowed these travellers to found their city in return for their worship in a nice piece of you-scratch-my-back-I'll-scratch-yours action.

Oshun shows there is no point being backward in coming forward and you have to ask for what you deserve, whether that's offerings and rituals from the people you allow to live near your river, or respect from the colleagues you created the world with. Oshun is a goddess who helps amplify women's voices, and you can find her mentioned in this capacity by the celebrated writer and activist Audre Lorde in her magnificent poem 'The Winds of Orisha'. Oshun is a great inspiration for making sure you prioritise self-respect while still looking out for other people around you. This glorious river goddess is overflowing with bounty.

Inanna
and Embracing Ambition

SUMERIAN, IRAQ

ALSO KNOWN AS

Queen of Heaven, Ishtar (in Babylon), Lady of the Date Clusters, Mistress of Heaven with the Great Pectoral Jewels

SKILLS

Fighting, Bravery, Wrath, Dispensing Divine Justice, Seduction, Standing on Lions

RESPONSIBILITIES

War, Truth, Godship, Music, Love, Sex, Politics, Power, Fertility (and as you'll see, many, many more)

When we think of female ambition, we think of that tired trope of a bitch businesswoman with boobs of steel, clambering without a backward glance over the still-twitching bodies of her colleagues in her ruthless pursuit of power. (They do tend to dress well though: think Cersei Lannister, Claire Underwood and Miranda Priestly.*) For men, ambition is associated with drive, success and confidence. The double standard is wearying, isn't it? What if we could move away from gendered stereotypes to find a way to harness our inner achievers without having to give a second thought to how people perceived us? Arch-goddess Inanna, Queen of Heaven herself, was worshipped across Ancient Mesopotamia. Her huge popularity belies the fact she sometimes got up to some extraordinary and frankly questionable antics in order to fulfil her ambitions.

In the fourth millennium BCE Mesopotamia was where it was at: all of human civilisation rested here, and successive cultures of Sumerians, Akkadians, Babylonians, Assyrians and Persians had shared mythologies, which overlapped and mirrored each other. Inanna, later known as Ishtar, was at the centre of many of them. Mesopotamians were the first urbanites

* Shiv Roy's a bit too fond of clingy neutrals and wide-leg trousers to make this list.

– they loved a metropolis and each city had its own god: Inanna's neighbourhood was the melodiously named Uruk. But their cities were fragile, plagued by the twin terrors of flood and drought, as well as war, and these very real threats lie at the heart of their mythology – a good example of the way humanity has always used stories to deal with tribulations it faces.

Inanna was the goddess of love, sex, beauty and desire, but also of war, fighting and politics. She's often depicted standing on a lion as a sign of her immense power. It's not difficult to see why she was so revered and adored; she's got a heady combo going on, which reflected the contradictions at the heart of Mesopotamian culture – a culture that could be benevolent and vicious, fearless and protective, all at the same time. Inanna features in more fables than any other Mesopotamian god or goddess, and many of the myths around her describe her demonstrating quite breathtaking ambition, often seizing control of other gods' territory with relish.

Inanna's father was Enki, god of water and also guardian of the *mes*, which in Sumerian mythology were the sacred powers doled out to various gods and goddesses so they could order the world and bring together civilisation. Inanna was not ready to settle with her apportioned *mes* selection (a pretty impressive spread of woodworking, metalworking, writing, building and basket-weaving, amongst others). She nursed an ambition to make her city and therefore herself even more of a powerhouse, so she set off in her heavenly boat to ask her dad Enki for more *mes*. She charms Enki and they sit down to have a nice dinner together. Essentially Inanna gets Pops extremely drunk, and as he slips further into the sauce he demonstrates more and more largesse – a by-product of booze many of us can recognise. When he wakes with a banging head he finds Inanna has vanished with more than a hundred *mes* that he's accidentally handed over to her. She's wangled some of the big guns: godship, the throne of kingship, truth, sex, wisdom, fear and music. Enki attempts to wrestle back the sacred job descriptions but Inanna calls HR and shames him into retreat; in a nimble feat of emotional blackmail she flips his anger into her hurt that he's rescinding his word, and summons her BFF, the warrior goddess Ninshubur, to fend him off.

Another famous story involves Inanna heading into the underworld in an attempt to seize it from her sister Ereshkigal, Queen of Hell. Inanna is married to a hot young shepherd-god called Dumuzi, whom she leaves at home while she gets on with the important business of usurping, telling Ninshubur to come and get her if she hasn't returned within three days. Inanna dresses up in her finest battle outfit, with each of her seven garments representing one of her *mes*. To get to Ereshkigal's palace she has to pass through seven gates in seven walls. At each one a gatekeeper demands she remove an item of clothing, so she finally arrives in front of her sister defenceless and starkers. Her attempted takedown is a disaster: she's sentenced to death and her cadaver is impaled on a spike as a warning to others. Ninshubur pleads with the other gods to intervene, but only Enki swoops in to rescue her and bring her back to life, loyal to his daughter despite her previous transgressions.

Inanna flees the underworld pursued by an army of devils who insist on taking someone as a replacement. Dumuzi has been living it up in her absence, lounging on her throne, surrounded by beautiful women (Dumb-uzi). Inanna is royally pissed off and sends her husband to the underworld to take her place. But in the end she does show an impressive level of compromise and forgiveness to her clearly-not-worth-it husband: a deal is struck where the holiday in hell is divided between Dumuzi and his blameless sister, the goddess of agriculture, Geshtinanna. Dumuzi will emerge into the upper worlds and return to Inanna and his corner office in spring, bringing growth and fertility, but in autumn he heads back down to the basement to do some filing – some might say Inanna's got herself the perfect relationship.

We can see strands of Inanna's descent in the later Greek myth of the harvest goddess Demeter and her daughter Persephone. Hades, king of the underworld, abducts his niece Persephone, forcing her to be his wife. When Demeter flips out about this and threatens to starve the world, he's persuaded to hand her back, but not before she has eaten six pomegranate seeds, which condemn her to spending six months of the year with her dismal husband below ground and six months above. *Et voilà!* We have the seasons.

We know so much about intoxicating Inanna because of the Sumerian priestess Enheduanna – humanity's first named author – who wrote hymns and poems dedicated to her, celebrating her beautiful, terrifying, awe-inspiring attributes. Inanna inspired complete devotion and loyalty because she could represent all elements of the spectrum from light to dark. We're not suggesting you charm, steal and confront your way to the top, as Inanna often did, but she's a powerful role model when it comes to the idea of envisioning your goals, preparing properly and showing determination in going for them – and also revelling in the praise your achievements bring. Too often women attribute their successes to luck or serendipity and instead we should look to own them, as Inanna did. So leave man-bition to the men, rip up the script and embrace your inner Inanna.

The Morrigan

and Being a Bitch

IRISH, IRELAND

ALSO KNOWN AS

The Great Queen, The Phantom Queen,
Badbh (crow), Macha (field),
Nemain (frenzy)

SKILLS

Prophecy, Shapeshifting, Sorcery,
Bickering, Upsetting Noises,
Causing Trouble, Laundering Armour

RESPONSIBILITIES

War, Death, Cows, Crows,
Horses, Territory

Many of our goddesses brim with inspiring positivity, healing and creative power and other sunny things associated with fertile femininity. But everything has its flipside and the Irish goddess the Morrígan is associated with far less cuddly attributes. She's more of a black-leather-and-*rouge-noir*-lipstick-making-inappropriate-comments-about-death-at-a-wedding kind of girl. The kind we like.

The Morrígan was a war goddess. (As with Hollywood and WWF favourite The Rock, the definite article in her name adds to her potent pugnacious vibe.) Her main pastimes included inciting violence and prophesying doom – she was great fun at parties. Her other hobbies were annoying the great mythological Irish hero Cú Chulainn (also known as 'the Hound', *Game of Thrones* fans) and sneakily disguising herself in different forms – frequently appearing as a carrion crow partial to feasting on the bodies of fallen warriors. All in all a stone-cold bitch – literally, as in one story she attacks Cú Chulainn in the form of a she-wolf. (Her other animagus outfits included an eel, a white heifer with red ears, a gorgeous young strumpet, an old crone and a red woman with red eyebrows driving a red chariot pulled by a one-legged red horse – committed colour-blocking.)

We know about the Morrígan from the *Táin Bó Cuailnge* (*Cattle Raid of Cooley*), part of the collection of Irish mythology known as the Ulster cycle. There is a great deal of thought-provoking stuff about the role of women in this story, not least because the raid it describes is instigated by the promiscuous Queen Medb of Connacht against her neighbours the Ulstermen, of whom only the teen Cú Chulainn is capable of putting up any resistance. This is because his compatriots have all been inconveniently cursed by the Morrígan in her personification as an athletic young woman called Macha: 'When things are toughest for you, those of you who guard this province will have only the strength of a woman in childbirth.' Macha pronounces this curse because she has been forced to race against the king's horses while pregnant with twins. She wins, impressively, but is so furious about her terrible and disrespectful treatment by the king and his men that she issues this game-changing malediction.

Celtic goddesses tended to be multitaskers and didn't always have clearly delineated areas of patronage. They also frequently appeared in more than one form. The Morrígan is a triple goddess who pops up in the personages of Badbh, Nemain and Macha – all of whom are involved in conflict and argy-bargy in some way. Her multiform nature is also expressed in her talent as a shapeshifter, often duping Cú Chulainn, who only realises who she is after they've pissed each other off. Despite the fact that war was a male occupation, the most prominent Irish war deities are female.* The Morrígan didn't, however, get down and dirty with hand-to-hand combat, taking on more of a shrieky cheerleading role.

Goddesses in many stories often function simply as obstacles or supporters of great heroes, and the Morrígan is both to Cú Chulainn. In different accounts she builds him up or cuts him down, but they rarely exchange a friendly word. She first appears to him as a beautiful young woman offering her help and partnership, which he refuses in a rather ungentlemanly way by saying he's busy and 'didn't come here for a woman's arse'. It's important to remember that immortals are frequently sensitive about being turned down for dates, but while gods tend to then just go ahead and rape people, goddesses often play the long game to make sure the hero in question has a really tough day at the office instead. In this instance the Morrígan messes things up for Cú Chulainn in his next battle by

* One of the coolest of these martial madams was the war goddess Scáthach, who was Cú Chulainn's personal trainer when he went to battle camp on the Isle of Skye. She would doubtless have been great on *SAS: Who Dares Wins*.

tripping him up while in the form of an eel and then causing chaos as a wolf and a rampaging heifer.

However, towards the end of Cú Chulainn's courageous combat career, the malevolent Ms M. in some accounts tries to protect him – in a typically frustrating way – by breaking his chariot to prevent him going into his final battle. As a prophetess, she knows his inevitable fate and she fills him in on this in full-on theatrical style. Casting off her previous incarnations, she appears in the form of an old lady washing his bloodied armour in a ford, and then as three more elderly dames who persuade him into eating some bad-luck dogmeat. It has to be said that the Morrígan fully embraced the dark goth horror-film vibe at all times.

Shallow water was seen as a place of contact with the Otherworld of the supernatural and this figure of the Washer at the Ford recurs in Scottish and French folklore, usually indicating the impending death of the person whose armour she is scrubbing with literal fairy liquid: 'Here and there around us are many bloody spoils; horrible are the huge entrails the Morrígan washes.' It's not a sight any soldier wants to see. When Cú Chulainn does finally meet his foretold bruising end, having tied himself to a stone on the battlefield so he can die standing up, the Morrígan lands on his shoulder in her form as a crow and this is how his enemies finally know he really is dead.

Despite the fact that she is described as instilling terror whenever she appears, particularly when emitting hideous battle cries before a skirmish (linking her with the famous Irish wailing spirits called banshees), there are more positive ways to interpret the Morrígan. A warrior's death was considered a glorious one and she is an instigator of this honour and success – her baiting of Cú Chulainn contributes to his legendary deeds.

So is the Morrígan a bitch? And are you? Beyond the veterinary female dog definition, 'bitch' can mean a woman who is malicious ('Carol told Layla I hate her shoes – what a bitch!'), a woman who is promiscuous ('That bitch Carol copped off with Alan behind my back'), a person who is under the thumb of someone else ('Alan is Carol's bitch'), and it's even sometimes used as a complimentary reference to someone's toughness ('Carol is one bad bitch!'). It's one of those words where the meaning is very much dependent on context and it feels different depending on whether it's said by a man or a woman. Obviously, being malicious is wrong, but this insult is thrown about quite casually when discussing women, even if they are completely malice-free. Behaviours that come across as authoritative in men are often interpreted (by both men and women) as cold and aggressive in women because we're indoctrinated to assume that women should be warm and womb-y and cuddly. That wasn't the Morrígan's bag at all. So if you are noisy and fierce in the defence of what's yours, if you meet disrespect with assertiveness, if you hook up with who you want for your own reasons, then it's likely someone will call you a bitch at some point – just like the Morrígan. But, just like her, it doesn't mean that you should give a damn.

Bastet
and the Power of Female Solidarity

EGYPTIAN, EGYPT

ALSO KNOWN AS

The Lady of Dread, The Lady of Life, The Lady of Slaughter, Lady of the East, The Goddess of the Rising Sun, The Sacred and All-Seeing Eye, Bast, Sekhmet

SKILLS

Protecting Women, Medicine, Having a Good Time

RESPONSIBILITIES

Love, Health, Fertility, Joy, Dance, Women, Secrets, War, Fire

Ancient Egypt was one of the very first grand human civilisations, and like their Mesopotamian contemporaries the Egyptians also had a multi-peopled belief system with a full roster of nature gods and goddesses. However, their approach to deities was dramatically different. Mesopotamians were at the mercy of extremely brutal forces of nature and aggressive wars. The rivers Tigris and Euphrates on which many city-states were built were prone to erratic flooding, and those city-states were often at war; consequently, they saw their deities as crazy-assed vengeful beings that needed to be appeased and grovelled to by priests in order to stop them wreaking havoc and disaster on their everyday existence.

For Ancient Egyptians, on the other hand, life was pretty sweet. Ancient Egypt occupied a tract of land along the Nile Valley in North Africa; the Nile flooded, sure, but in such an orderly fashion that they were able to build their calendar around it. Their gods were merciful bestowers of gifts like wisdom and truth, and the afterlife was even more blissful than the present one. (Of course, this sense of well-being clearly didn't pervade for those at the bottom of the pile, like slaves.) The Pharaoh was the earthly incarnation of the sky god Horus and therefore representative of the central value of *ma'at* – harmony and equilibrium in every aspect of life, including between the sexes.

In Ancient Egypt, a person's rights were based on social standing, rather than gender – women of high status could occupy significant roles and enjoyed similar freedoms and protections as men in the same social strata. Women had the right to an education – there were famous female artists, doctors and entertainers – and it stayed that way until the Greek occupation in 332 BCE. This was reflected too in a roster of all-powerful goddesses. One of the most beloved of all the gods, male or female, was Bastet, who came to prominence during the rule of the Second Dynasty, which began around 2890 BCE. She is closely associated with Sekhmet, the savage, lion-headed daughter of the sun god Ra, who acted as protector of the Pharaohs. Sekhmet was more feral than her later personification as Bastet and was a kind of hit-woman for Ra. Once when he asked her to take out some undesirables she became so frenzied that she couldn't stop slaughtering people until Ra dyed some beer red to convince her it was human blood and she passed out from drinking it. Over time she morphed into a more benign, cat-headed goddess, who was associated with the home, fertility and women's secrets.

Now, anyone who's watched *Mean Girls* or read Jane Austen can attest to the fact that sometimes between women, it's complicated. But Bastet is an icon who really does always have women's backs. She was a protector of the domestic sphere, and fender-off of evil spirits and diseases, particularly those that affected children and women. She was also associated with perfume and olfactory euphoria.

The Egyptians really, really loved cats. Some scholars think that they had a law that meant a death sentence if you killed a cat, even by accident.* Think how much they would have loved Cats of Instagram or LOLcats! Cats weren't just appreciated as snuggly buddies, however; they were revered as sacred in

* 'In ancient times cats were worshipped as gods; they have not forgotten this': Terry Pratchett.

Ancient Egypt because they killed the mice and snakes that brought disease and threatened crops, and also apparently helped on hunting trips (this is a testament to the skills of their Egyptian owners, who could literally herd cats). The cats that lived in Bastet's temple in Bubastis, the ruins of which still survive today, were specially protected and stylishly mummified after their deaths.

There are many stories of Bastet's bravery and protection of women, but our favourite is her role in a cautionary tale from the Ancient Egyptian cycle *The Tales of Prince Setna*. The impulsive young Prince Setna enters a tomb looking for a magical book, which he plans to pilfer. He's confronted by ghosts who guard it but ignores their pleas and nabs it anyway. Shortly after, he spies a drop-dead gorgeous woman, Taboubu, a priestess of Bastet, with whom he becomes immediately sexually obsessed – she's his own personal catnip. He sends her a note offering her ten gold pieces if she'll visit him in his bed; she counter-offers, telling him to come to the temple where she lives.

A horny Setna shows up at Taboubu's door, but before he can get her in the sack, she says he must sign over all his possessions in a sort of ancient pre-nup. He agrees, but then she says she needs all his children there to witness the signing so that there's no court battle. Again, he is so pumped he agrees, and while they're signing Taboubu slips into a diaphanous dress, pushing him over the edge, so that when she finally requests that his children be murdered, he acquiesces. They begin to get down to it when Taboubu screams and vanishes, along with the bedroom they are in and all his clothes, so that Setna is left on the street, naked, with his penis stuck in a clay pot. At which point the Pharaoh drives past as a witness to his complete humiliation – and informs him the whole thing has been a mirage. A sorry Setna realises he must return the book and stop annoying the ghosts. Scholars view Taboubu as a representation of Bastet – her wind-up of Setna is just like a cat toying with a mouse – and the story speaks to Bastet's role as a punisher of people who pissed around with the gods. It's also a stern lesson to men not to view women merely as sexual objects.

Followers of Bastet knew how to have a good time. Ancient historian Herodotus describes extremely fun-sounding scenes at her feast, which was celebrated annually at Bubastis. Hundreds of thousands of men and women (mainly women, though, leaving the kids at home) travelled to Bubastis to drink, make wild music and flash their bits – a mass mooning that symbolised the casting off of everyday norms, and a wink to Bastet's powers of fertility. Intriguingly, Bastet was as popular amongst men as she was with women – so popular, in fact, that during one invasion, the marauding Persian army painted her on their shields, knowing their opposition couldn't bring themselves to attack the image of their beloved Bastet.

So reconfigure any ideas you might have about cat ladies: Bastet is the ultimate in feline fellowship and feminine protection. A mass mooning might be a step too far as an expression of solidarity (though it could be fun), but there is undeniable power in sticking together and supporting one another – rather than adhering to the lonely 'Only Girl' or 'Cool Girl' tropes.* And make sure you are supporting all different kinds of women in your mutual-support group hug, not just those most like you. So do your research to make sure your feminism is intersectional, hand out the dancer emojis to all the amazing women around you,** big up your colleagues when they deliver the goods, compliment another woman on her smile, her style or her smarts. And then sit back and watch them purr.

* In which you cast yourself as not like other women and probably not liking other women, recoil from the notion of feminism and cheer on misogyny in an attempt to grab power by association by being seen as 'one of the guys' – it's quite hard work.

** Or try Bastet's own emoji/hieroglyph. (The first icon in her name is a perfume jar showing her connection with scent.)

Fortuna
and Making Your Own Luck

CLASSICAL, ITALY

ALSO KNOWN AS

Tyche, Eutykhia, Nemesis, Fors, Felicitas, Fortuna Bona (good luck), Fortuna Muliebris (women's fortune), Fortuna Huiusce Diei (today's fortune), Fortuna Balnearis (fortune of the baths/health), Fortuna Redux (the fortune of return – for soldiers) and many others

SKILLS

Bringing Good Luck or Bad Luck, Keeping Everyone Guessing

RESPONSIBILITIES

Favouring the Bold, Guarding Cities

The Roman goddess Fortuna is thought to have begun her auspicious career in ancient Italy as an agricultural goddess who brought fertility and prosperity. Later she became mixed up with the Greek goddess of luck and fortune, Tyche. Both Tyche and Fortuna are hard deities to pin down. In fact, the only thing you can actually bet on with Lady Luck is her inconsistency. And though this might seem counter-intuitive, it may be the very fact that you can't depend on her at all that provides us with the best lesson she can teach us today.

Tyche was said to be one of the three thousand daughters of Oceanus and Tethys, who were part of the divine family known as the Titans, who ruled the cosmos before being usurped by the more slebby Olympian gods led by Zeus. Stories and depictions of Tyche are all about ambivalence: sometimes she's good, sometimes she's bad, and ultimately she's unchangeably changeable. When she was in a good mood Tyche was worshipped as Eutykhia, or good fortune, but she was also associated with Nemesis, the goddess of retribution, there to bring you down if you become arrogant due to all your lovely good fortune. If there's one thing the gods hate, it's hubris.

Tyche and Fortuna were portrayed as blind, and often with wings, signifying the unbiased and flighty

nature of chance. Both of them often carry a cornucopia showing off all the great goodies they can bring if they fancy it and also the more eccentric accessory of a rudder, symbolising the way they navigate destiny. They are sometimes shown balancing on a ball to show the instability of fate, and how fortune and luck can shift the very ground you stand on in a heartbeat.* They make for an ambitious fancy-dress costume.

Tyche's popularity in Greece grew under the extraordinary winning streak of the warrior king Alexander the Great during the fourth century BCE, and she was the patron goddess of many cities, portrayed on coins and jewellery (could this be where flipping a coin to let the gods decide all began?). Similarly, Fortuna flourished when the Roman Empire was having a good old go at conquering the world in the first century CE. It was during this time that the Roman writer Pliny** wrote about her dominance, 'All over the world, in all places and at all times, Fortuna is the only god whom everyone invokes; she alone is in our thoughts; is praised

* Tyche and Fortuna have a much more active circus-skills vibe than those other famous classical goddesses of destiny, the Fates. These three old-lady sisters spent their time on sinister needlework, spinning out the threads of people's lives and cutting them at their deaths. They are more big-picture than Tyche and Fortuna, and even the other gods have to follow the ultimate destiny they spin.

** In an instance of extreme *bad* luck, Pliny died in 79 CE while trying to rescue some mates from the eruption of Mount Vesuvius.

and blamed and loaded with reproaches; wavering as she is, conceived by the generality of mankind to be blind, wandering, inconstant, uncertain, variable and often favouring the unworthy. To her are referred all our losses and all our gains.'

Fortuna also plays a crucial role in Rome's self-aggrandising foundation myth. The writer and thinker Plutarch gives Fortuna credit for making sure that the she-wolf who suckled Romulus and Remus had plenty of milk and didn't gobble them up. To recap: Romulus and Remus were twin boys, heirs to the throne of a kingdom in Italy, whose usurping uncle attempted to get rid of them. They were dumped on the banks of the Tiber to perish, but saved by the famous she-wolf you can still see suckling them on merch all over Rome today. When the boys grew up they went to the seven hills that are now part of Rome to found their own city, but disagreed on which hill they should build. In the kick of sibling rivalry, Romulus ended up killing Remus and Rome was born.* Lucky old Romulus had Fortuna on his side at this crucial moment too.

One of the first of many temples dedicated to Fortuna was set up by the early Roman king Servius Tullius, who ruled Rome in the sixth century BCE,

* If the other twin had won the fratricidal spat, the city would be called Reme, which doesn't sound as good.

hundreds of years pre-Empire. Tullius' mum was a slave, but he married the king's daughter, and his rags-to-riches tale was much admired by less fortunate citizens. It's not surprising that slaves loved Fortuna – she could bring great success, even when the odds were stacked against you. Similarly, working women and prostitutes had a special celebration for a specific aspect of Fortuna called Fortuna Virilis (Manly Fortune) on 1 April each year, when they all met up for some kind of secret spa day in the men's public baths.

Fortuna isn't just a goddess for winners. She was also held accountable when the shit hit the fan. Rome endured many sackings over the centuries but its first, by the Gauls in 390 BCE, was probably the most terrifying. The Romans hadn't yet perfected their fearsome fighting style, so stood by while terrifying Gaulish warriors raped, pillaged and generally dicked over their city. Eventually, the Romans paid them a thousand pounds of gold to give it a rest and leave them alone. The Roman historian Livy wrote of his city folks' unpreparedness: 'Such is the blindness Fortune visits on men's minds when she would have her gathering might meet with no check.'

It's interesting how Fortuna's iconography has survived over the centuries: of all the classical goddesses she has real staying power. She certainly didn't disappear when Christianity rolled into town and was super-popular in the Middle Ages, but instead appeared in lots of works of art with her natty, random-spinning Wheel of Fortune. Many different religions encompass ideas of divine providence: Japan's Kichijōten is often depicted holding a handy wish-granting pearl, and the Thai luck goddess, Nang Kwak, holds a bag of gold – statues of her are found in shops that hope to attract good business. Both are related to the Hindu, Jain and Buddhist goddess Lakshmi, who is also associated with prosperity and good fortune and carries a lotus flower; Lakshmi is celebrated at the annual festival of Diwali.

Even today, Fortuna is a symbol of our most keenly felt hopes, desires, dreams and fears and the unpredictability of what comes to us. But there's a different, more proactive way to think about luck, one which acknowledges the role we each play in our own destiny. Luck is defined as success or failure influenced by chance. How you interpret and deal with the slings and arrows life throws your way shapes your future. You can make your own luck by being brave, by taking chances and risks, and not being afraid of failure.

Life is full of sliding-door moments where, if you hadn't thrown the dice, or spun the wheel, things might have turned out differently. That date with the girl with bad shoes you'd discounted at first? What if she turns out to be the best thing that's ever happened to you? That outlier candidate for a job in your team? What if she comes in and shakes everything up for the better? Studies suggest that people who consider themselves lucky tend to get better luck – probably because they interpret everything that happens as an opportunity. Life can be a crap shoot, so grab the best of what it offers. Be flexible, be nimble, be prepared to be wrong. And remember that if you find yourself on a losing streak the most predictable thing about life (or luck) is that it will at some point change. As Plutarch said, 'Swift is the pace of Fortune, bold is her spirit, and most vaunting her hopes.'

White Buffalo Calf Woman
and Respect

LAKOTA, NORTH AMERICA

ALSO KNOWN AS

Pte San Win

SKILLS

Wisdom, Communication, Fatal Cloud Deployment, Prophecy

RESPONSIBILITIES

Sacred Rituals, Buffalo, The Interconnected World

R-E-S-P-E-C-T is a crucial concept to nurture in our divided times. It may conjure images of a Victorian father demanding that his children call him 'sir' or politicians saying 'with *respect*' when they mean the exact opposite, but considered properly it is a powerful concept, and one that goes well beyond the boundaries of minding your Ps and Qs. The word 'respect' draws in cosy ideas of gratitude, value and trust but also more steely concepts like admiration, honour and appropriate deference. As a society, we like to think we're getting better at respecting human rights, whether that is the rights of women, children, LGBTQI+ people, people of colour or those with disabilities, but this hasn't always been the case and we've still got a long way to go. There is also a lot to think about in terms of the reverence we show towards non-human life on our planet.

White Buffalo Calf Woman is a mythical figure whose story is bound up with ideas of respect on many levels, from the personal to the communal, the spiritual and the ecological. She is considered a supernatural prophetess by the Lakota people of North America, and her story also appears in the mythology of other indigenous peoples who inhabit the same area of the Great Plains, in the middle of the USA. She first appeared to impart her wisdom many hundreds of years ago and promised

to return again in the future.* Her story is still passed down through generations as part of the rich and essential oral storytelling tradition of her people.

There is no unified indigenous North American mythology because the nations and peoples that are gathered under this term are so varied and distinct: there were over four hundred different cultures and language groups spread out over North America before white people arrived and there are 574 federally recognised tribes just in the USA today. Early written English recordings of oral tales, transcribed well after colonisation and Christianisation began, cannot fully translate the meanings that the various versions of the White Buffalo Calf Woman narrative had or has for Lakota listeners.

Despite the focus of the average school textbook, the American continent was inhabited long before Christopher Columbus landed in 1492. The original peoples of the Americas have lived there for at least fifteen thousand years and have contributed hugely to our world today: 60 per cent of the world's food

* Mythology boffins call figures who teach humans something important about the world, often saving it from disaster, 'culture heroes'. Jesus and King Arthur are culture heroes who, like White Buffalo Calf Woman, are prophesied to return in the future, which would make for an interesting dinner party if they all arrived at once. Culture *heroines* are less common than heroes, but in this book the Wawilak Sisters and Sedna fit this category.

sources come from plants first developed by them, which is pretty gobsmacking. But outsiders' concepts of indigenous American life have focused on interaction with European Americans, who imposed centuries of conflict and brutal suppression as they 'discovered' the 'new continent'. Since first contact, indigenous North American culture has been subject to massive disrespect in what is now the USA: take your pick from the violence of warfare, over five hundred broken government treaties, territorial invasion and forced relocations of the nineteenth century; the oppressive assimilation policies, religious suppression and separation of families in the twentieth century; or the ongoing discrimination and simplistic and outdated portrayals in the media. In fact, it's rare to find TV or films which include contemporary Native American characters at all: a recent First Nations Development Institute study of over thirteen thousand people found that the invisibility of contemporary Native American experiences and concerns in education and the media was one of the most significant barriers to understanding between Native and non-Native communities.

The first European contact with the people of the Great Plains occurred in the mid-sixteenth century but it was the growth of the fur trade and pioneers heading west in the nineteenth century that brought travellers and settlers onto Lakota land without permission. When conflict arose, treaties were signed between the US government and the local tribes, including one that granted the territory of the Black Hills to the indigenous people in perpetuity. However, this didn't stop General Custer tipping up in 1874 on a mission to see whether there was any gold in them there hills. His success meant the government turned a blind eye to the influx of miners who descended on Lakota land in their thousands to dig it up.

From this point on, the US Army made increasingly aggressive efforts to support settlers and remove Native Americans from their ancestral territory and contain them in reservations, often far from their original homes and on inhospitable land. They were also banned from engaging in many of their sacred rituals. The resulting hostilities in the Black Hills led to the Battle of the Greasy Grass (also known as the Battle of Little Bighorn) in 1876, where Custer and his regiment tried to force various bands to move to reservations but were decimated by fighters including the famous Lakota warrior Crazy Horse. The ensuing wars of resistance on the Plains ended with the horrifying massacre at Wounded Knee in December 1890, when hundreds of Lakota, including many women and children, were killed by US Army forces.

One of the strategies used to force the Lakota onto reservations was denying them access to food – in the end they had to choose compliance over starvation. Government forces slaughtered their prime source of nourishment and equipment, the buffalo, so effectively that by 1890 millions of buffalo had been hunted to near extinction, with just a few hundred left. This caused a huge change in the Plains ecosystem but also placed great physical and spiritual strain on the Lakota, for whom the buffalo are sacred. Buffalo were honoured with rituals to thank them for allowing themselves to be hunted for food and supplies; for their formidable physical fortitude (which consequently also endowed prestige on those who hunted them skilfully); and for their connection to both the people and Wakan Tanka (often translated as the Great Spirit), which animates all aspects of the universe.

The story of White Buffalo Calf Woman highlights the powerful connection between the Lakota and buffalo. It tells of a Lakota group called the Itazipcho who were travelling and looking for food in a time of scarcity. Two scouts encountered a woman with striking eyes in a white buffalo-hide dress who seemed to float towards them carrying a bundle and a bunch of sage, with red marks on her face and long dark hair with one strand tied with buffalo hide. One of the scouts immediately took a fancy to her and, despite his associate's protestations, attempted to assault her. Immediately a dark cloud descended and covered them and when it lifted all that was left of the aggressor were his bones on the ground; he had been consumed by rattlesnakes. After reassuring the remaining scout, the woman instructed him to tell his people to prepare for her arrival.

The Itazipcho built a special tipi and altar for White Buffalo Calf Woman as she requested, and when she arrived they greeted her with respectful hospitality and offered her water, which was pretty much all they had. In return she presented them with the *chanunpa*, or sacred pipe, which from this point on became the most important ritual object for the Lakota. (The *chanunpa* given by White Buffalo Calf Woman has been handed down through generations and is currently kept by Chief Arvol Looking Horse. Chief Looking Horse is a celebrated environmental campaigner: in 2019 he met with Greta Thunberg along with the young Lakota environmental activist Tokata Iron Eyes.) She also taught them other central ceremonies, which are still practised. She praised the men, children and women of the group, telling the women, 'You are from Mother Earth. What you are doing is as great as the warriors do,' stressing the unity of the community working together and also the unity of all creation: 'Wakan Tanka smiles upon us because now we are as one: earth, sky, all living things, the two-legged, the four-legged, the winged ones, the trees, the grasses. Together with the people, they are all related, one family.' This principle of interconnectedness is central to Lakota philosophy.

When she left, White Buffalo Calf Woman walked into the setting sun and changed form four times, first into a black buffalo calf, then brown, then red, then finally white. White buffalo are extremely rare and are considered harbingers of White Buffalo Calf Woman's return, which will bring harmony to the world. Cultivating mutual respect is one way in which we can strive towards this harmony. White Buffalo Calf Woman not only demanded respect for her own physical person, but also asked the people she visited to respect the contributions of one another and the sacred rites which tie them to all creation. Her message, although directed at and precious to a specific community, is one we can all learn from in the hope of a better future – through showing greater respect both for the environment and for each other.

We live in a time of fierce public debate and strongly held opinions, so sometimes it's hard to identify the connective tissue which links us all. It takes discipline and thoughtfulness to approach each other with a default attitude of respect. So the next time you are tempted to fire off a hot take or join in with some group castigation on social media: think about White Buffalo Calf Woman's message, take a deep breath and show some respect.

Baba Yaga
and Being Unapologetic

SLAVIC, RUSSIA

ALSO KNOWN AS

Baba Iaga, Forest Mother

SKILLS

Testing People, Kidnapping Children, Bold Interior Decoration, Scaring the Bejaysus Out of Folk, Flying, Cooking with Humans

RESPONSIBILITIES

The Seasons, The Forest, Death, Occult Knowledge

Wild, unkempt, snakey, revolting hair: yes. Huge hooked nose that is said to skim the ceiling while she sleeps: yup. Flying pestle and mortar as a mode of supernatural transport: bring it on. House that roosts atop huge dancing, shuffling chicken legs, surrounded by a fence made of glowing skulls, and a slurpy penchant for eating those

who come to seek her advice: *hell* yes. The Baba Yaga, the most famous witch of Russian folklore, lives by her own rules and apologises to no one.

'Sorry' has become such a loaded word. We are all guilty of its overuse – see the particularly British habit of apologising when someone steps on your foot and steals your wallet (it's happened, we've witnessed it). We're not suggesting that men are incapable of the 's' word, but it's a fact that women do use it more, indicating something rather darker might be at play in our rush to apologise.

'Sorry''s evil twin is 'No worries if not!', which is often used, again mainly by women, to suggest a breezy diffidence, usually as a protective mechanism against rejection. 'Well, yes, I would really like that payrise you promised and which I have worked my arse off for, but no worries if not!'; 'Yes, perhaps after three years of sharing a flat and life goals it is time to meet your parents, but no worries if not!'; 'Yes, it's been a long time since our last night out with some wine and good convo, but I do understand you can't have even one second away from your children, so no worries if not!' Language is powerful, and words that cushion like this can end up being self-fulfilling: projecting a lack of confidence can inspire just that.

The Baba Yaga wouldn't stand for any of this kind

of nonsense. She is a fabulously horrific hag who lives in the forest in her very own off-grid ghoulish grand design, assisted by her faithful servants, three pairs of disembodied hands. Baba Yaga's worth isn't tied to others – she has no romantic relationships: even when she is described as having daughters there is never a father involved. She resists all traditional ideas of beauty and constraint. She is a brilliant agent of subversion: for Baba Yaga even kitchen utensils are weaponised; note her huge flying pestle and mortar. She makes women's ordinary domestic objects powerful and unnerving. She is gloriously, entirely other.

Baba is a shapeshifter, resisting all forms of categorisation: she can appear as a snake, a bird, and at harvest time she lives in the last sheaf of grain as a symbol of fertility. She is a wild woodland woman and 'Mistress of Beasts', like the Greek goddess Artemis (but much less glam). In stories concerning Baba Yaga she is depicted either as a maternal mentor or as a bloodthirsty baddie* – in this again she's an unusual figure from folklore, in that even her archetype shifts. In her most famous story, 'Vasilisa the Beautiful', she occupies both

* Keanu Reeves' hitman character in the *John Wick* films is referred to as Baba Yaga, bringing to mind the threat of something supernaturally scary that children are told will come for them if they are bad. It's nice that the filmmakers thought an old lady was the scariest possible thing a buff assassin could be likened to.

roles simultaneously. Vasilisa is a Cinderella type whose mother dies when she's a child. As she slips away, the mother gives her a special doll, promising it will give her guidance. Soon Vasilisa's father remarries. Her horrible stepmother (a rich fairytale archetype which could fill another book) brings with her two daughters and they all come to hate the kind and lovely Vasilisa. They treat her terribly and eventually plan to have her killed.

When Vasilisa's father is away on business the stepmother moves her family to the edge of a birch forest. They claim the fire in their house has gone out and send Vasilisa into the forest to ask Baba Yaga for a spark to help them survive – knowing most who look for the witch end up in her pot. Vasilisa is terrified, but her magic doll guides her as she makes her way through the spooky woods. When she arrives, Baba Yaga sets her a series of seemingly impossible domestic tasks – like separating a million poppy seeds from a pile of dust, which Vasilisa, with the help of her magic doll, manages to achieve. Mission accomplished, the Baba Yaga sends Vasilisa packing armed with new knowledge and the courage to ask questions, and with one of her glowing skull lanterns from her eclectic interior decor.

At home, her step-family are horrified that she's made it out alive, but put on a good show and fawn over their brave Vasilisa. The skull knows better though, sees them for what they are and incinerates them. The next morning Vasilisa wakes to three small piles of ash. Free from the shackles of her bloodsucking family, Vasilisa ends up marrying the Tsar, no less.

In the story Baba Yaga is both nemesis and saviour to Vasilisa as she undergoes a rite of passage. She journeys from browbeaten servant to fire-wielding agent of retribution; and Baba Yaga, terrifying though she is, enables the process. Some interpretations have the doll as representative of Vasilisa's instinct: she has to learn to listen to it, rather than meekly and apologetically accepting the lot that life has thrown at her. Baba Yaga forces her into a position where, alone and in the wild, she *has* to listen to her gut.

So what can we learn from the fearsome and bold Baba Yaga? In her refusal to accept any societal norms, much less apologise for being exactly who she is, Baba Yaga is the best kind of witch: full of knowledge, powerful and dangerous. So rather than using 'sorry' as a get-out clause, try to own your mistakes and offer solutions. Good practice at work is to simply stop using the word, especially in emails – instead of 'Sorry I didn't attach the document,' try 'I didn't attach the document, here it is now.' We need to teach ourselves not to shrink. We need to stop apologising for our age, for the shape of our bodies, for our achievements. We need to stop saying, 'Oh, this old thing,' 'It's nothing, really,' and start taking ownership instead. It's hard to be really bloody good at your job, to keep friendships and relationships on track, just as it's hard to balance work and life. We should not apologise for this. Use Baba Yaga as your #lifegoal instead: it's spell-binding stuff.

Aphrodite
and Understanding Love

CLASSICAL, GREECE

ALSO KNOWN AS

Venus (in Ancient Rome), Cytherea (born in Cythera), Cypris (or maybe born in Cyprus), Ourania (heavenly), Aphrodite Pandemos (for everyone), Aphrodite Philommeides (smile-loving), Chrysi (the golden), Euploia (good sailing), Kallipygos (nice arse) and many more

SKILLS

Matchmaking, Looking Great, Persuasion, Mixing Stuff Up

RESPONSIBILITIES

Love, Fertility, Sex, Pleasure, Sex Workers, Beauty, The Sea, Rome

Mighty Aphrodite is one of the world's most celebrated goddesses. When you call someone a 'goddess', you are probably thinking of her. Artists and sculptors through the ages have never tired of depicting her famous beauty and sexiness. She pretty much became an excuse to draw naked ladies, given her popularity as a mythological subject for male artists. To be fair, love – which is her area of expertise – is a perennial subject of fascination and exploration for humans; there aren't many books, films or songs that don't refer to it. And Aphrodite herself, as the personification of the power of love, continues to draw a crowd: there's a Kylie album named after her, Lady Gaga has sung about her in her Roman form as Venus, and her symbolic bird, the dove, graces a bestselling soap brand. You'll also see references to her mischievous archer son Eros everywhere on 14 February, in the arrows that so often pierce hearts on V Day cards.*

Aphrodite worship is thought by many scholars to have arrived in Greece from the East as a version of the cult of the great Mesopotamian goddess Inanna,

* Eros governs desire – which is why those films are called 'erotic movies'. His amorous gang of mates, the Erotes, include Anteros (mutual love), Pothos (longing) and Himeros (urgent desire). There were probably also loads more, like Metheros (drunk desire), Plexeros (bored desire) and Phoberos (he's-just-not-that-into-you desire), but we've just made these last three up.

who also liked doves and sex. Some scholars see Aphrodite's designation as a hyper-feminine 'goddess of love' as a simplification of her original ancient form, in which she was associated with war and primarily defined as having power over mixing and unifying people through sexual bonds. Her image has changed through the ages, through literature and her cult followers' interpretations, so she is a goddess of many parts. The myth of her rather unusual birth is one of the most famous of her stories.

When the Titan Cronos was busy overthrowing the original king of the gods, Ouranos (before he himself was overthrown by his own son Zeus – happy families!), he rather brutally cut off Ouranos' junk and threw it in the sea. The foam that resulted from Ouranos' bits plunging into the ocean transformed into the gorgeous goddess we know from Botticelli's famous painting, calmly surfing to shore on a shell with perfect windblown beachy waves in her hair. (Fair enough that the great Renaissance painter should choose this moment in Aphrodite's emergence rather than the less picturesque precursor.)

Aphrodite went on to become one of the top twelve Olympian gods* and appears in many myths, which

* In no particular order: 1. Zeus, serial rapist king god with thunderbolt; 2. His wife Hera, widely considered to be a right bitch but had her

usually show her sneaky ability to get her end away or cause trouble – matching the tenacious effects of love and desire and the way they can often mess things up.

One of these stories tells of how Aphrodite was copping off with the himbo god of war, Ares, when she was discovered by her husband Hephaestus. Hephaestus was gifted at crafts and knitted a net of gold, which he suspended above her bed, using it to trap the illicit couple when they got together. He then invited all the other Olympians round to laugh at them. It is quite likely that love will be the cause of some of the most embarrassing moments of your life, but this doesn't mean it's not worth pursuing (but make sure to choose someone more worthwhile than Ares).

However far Aphrodite stepped outside the rules of good behaviour required of mortal women in her time, she remained beloved and although she scandalised

reasons; 3. Athena, goddess of wisdom, war and being a man's woman (see pp. 1–7); 4. Poseidon, trident-wielding bolshy sea god; 5. Hephaestus, disabled volcano and metalworking god; 6. Artemis, singleton moon goddess of hunting; 7. Her twin bro, Apollo, high-achieving god of truth, art, healing and thinking he's better than you; 8. Ares, jock god of violence (one of those Wolverine/Hulk types with anger-management issues); 9. Demeter, motherly agriculture goddess; 10. Hermes, slippery messenger of the gods; 11. Dionysus, boozy god of getting off your nuts; 12. Our Aph. Interesting that of the four female Olympians, two are virgins, one is mumsy, one is often referred to as a harridan and one a whore. Between them they encompass influential outdated male stereotypes about what women are like.

the early Christians who transcribed a lot of the literature we have about her, she is seen today as a symbol of female sexual liberation. She had a lot of boyfriends and a lot of children by a lot of different guys, including Harmonia (harmony), Phobos (fear) and Demos (people) with Ares; Hermaphroditus with Hermes (who became the first ever intersex person); and Priapus (who became the first ever person to suffer from priapism) with Dionysus. She was also the mother of the Trojan hero Aeneas, who had a mortal father. After the fall of Troy, Aeneas sailed to Italy where he founded the settlement that would eventually become Rome under his descendant Romulus, so in her Latin form as Venus* she was a very significant goddess for the Romans.

Aphrodite is often considered a frivolous goddess. She *did* cause a lot of trouble – you can totally imagine her Villanelleing around in a Molly Goddard pink dress creating havoc. Sexy women have always caused a lot of anxiety amongst men: their very desirability makes them dangerous – and what if they turn out not to be silly after all and ice-pick you while you're in

* Venus is just as lovely as Aphrodite, and may have started out as an ancient Italian goddess of gardens, springtime and strawberries before being combined with her Greek sister, but now has the dubious honour of having given us the word 'venereal' to refer to sexually transmitted diseases.

bed? Aphrodite's mischief includes starting the Trojan War by fixing up the married Greek Helen with the Trojan Paris; giving the ladies of the island of Lemnos terrible BO for neglecting her shrines; and making Phaedra fall in love with her stepson Hippolytus. All of these acts resulted in terrible bloodshed, reflecting Aphrodite's ongoing link to Ares: love can lead to misguided anger or violence just as much as it can be the solution to them (it makes sense that one of their kids is called 'Fear' and one is 'Harmony'). The love goddess herself wasn't immune to her own painful power, however, as the famous story of her passion for the mortal Adonis shows.

Adonis was by all accounts the most gorgeous man ever and Aphrodite fell for him hard. She experienced the pain of lost love when he was gored to death by a boar on a hunting trip – the tears she shed over his body became the first anemone flowers. In some versions, the murderous hog was sent after her boyfriend by the goddess Artemis, who was cross about Aphrodite getting her own favourite, Hippolytus, killed. (Aphrodite took offence at Hippolytus because he dedicated himself to celibacy and Artemis instead of a life of love with her.) However, as well as the pain love can incite Aphrodite also brings people together in a positive way and has a protective aspect, even getting injured herself during the Trojan War while protecting her son Aeneas.

But what about the fixation on Aphrodite's beauty and glamour? Her fancy jewellery and riding about on swans and her constant failure to keep her clothes on? Isn't she just another example of the impossible standards and the accessibility of female bodies required to make them desirable?* Isn't she a shallow goddess who is only concerned with her own pleasure? A lot of airtime has certainly been given to Aphrodite's wondrous décolletage. (This is thanks to her techie hubby's special lingerie: Hephaestus made her a magical bra** that made her irresistible to all men, which seems somewhat self-defeating.) In Homer's *Iliad* there is a scene where she disguises herself as an old lady to try to persuade Helen to sleep with Paris, but Helen recognises her because of her splendid boobs. Aphrodite is certainly a goddess who uses her looks as leverage to get what she wants, and what she wants isn't always ethical. But don't hate her just because she's hot.

* If you look at famous depictions of Aphrodite her physique is probably less fashionable these days than an Artemis-style athleticism, which just goes to show that ideas of beauty and the ideal body image are not absolute and change all the time.

** Usually referred to, unappetisingly, as a 'girdle', this appears to have been a strap that ran under and between the boobs to keep them perky.

Beyond this focus on her external attributes Aphrodite is a very inclusive goddess.

The Ancient Greek philosopher Plato distinguished between two of Aphrodite's aspects, calling the one in charge of intellectual love Ourania (from the sky), and the other in charge of physical love Pandemos (for all people). Aphrodite Ourania was originally only concerned with love between men. Aphrodite is not just about feminine heterosexual desire: she looked after both hetero- and homosexual love and in later Roman times was worshipped by some as an intersex or androgynous deity called Venus Barbata (bearded Venus). Plenty of ancient mythologies show less anxiety about circumscribing gender than we encounter in our own times. In many cultures the creator deity is of no gender or both. There are also many gods who exist outside traditional gender norms, such as the Chinese Taoist deity Lan Caihe, who appears sometimes as a man and sometimes as a woman and sometimes dressed as a woman but with a man's voice; the Hindu goddess Minakshi, who was born with three breasts and brought up as a boy; the Egyptian god of the Nile's floods, Hapi, who is usually depicted as a male with breasts; the shape-shifting A-list Norse god Loki, who chooses whether he wants to be male or female in any given circumstance and is both father and mother to various kids; and the

Vodou father spirit, Baron Samedi, who is often depicted as wearing a mixture of traditionally male and female formalwear, and whose gender and sexuality are interpreted variously in different traditions.

In encompassing variety, Aphrodite is also not just about hearts-and-flowers romantic love (although she does especially like roses, anemones and myrtle). She also shows love for herself and attention to her own needs and encompasses parental affection (for Aeneas and Eros particularly) and general social bonding. With her entourage of Erotes, and her gal pals the Horai (the Seasons) and the Kharites (the Graces), she is a very sociable goddess, bringing people of all different kinds together. She looks after kings and emperors and sex workers and sailors. All of this amounts to a goddess of unity in diversity; an embracing, many-splendoured deity who reflects love in all its different forms, with all the pain, challenges and benefits that opening yourself up to love brings.

We all fixate on romantic love but don't be deceived into thinking that's the be-all and end-all. As Aphrodite shows, love can grow from the least promising beginnings and be whatever you make it: trouble, joy, family, spirituality, intellectual passion, self-respect. As the Greek philosopher Empedocles said, 'Love is innate to humans and because of her their thoughts are friendly and they work together, giving her the name Joy as well as Aphrodite.' Sometimes Aphrodite can be scary, but don't close yourself off to all that she can bring. Love is all you need.

Pachamama
and Finding Balance

INCA, SOUTH AMERICA

ALSO KNOWN AS

Mother Nature, Mother of the Universe, Old Woman of the Forest

SKILLS

Creativity, Making the Earth Move

RESPONSIBILITIES

Agriculture, Animals, Plants

Across cultures far and wide, and periods of history near and far, the most popular realms ruled by female deities have been nature and the earth: from Ancient Greek Gaia to Egyptian Isis, Sumerian Ninhursag with her lion cub, the great Maori mother goddess Papatūānuku, Hindu and Buddhist cosmic cow goddess Prithvi and the Chinese soil goddess Hòutǔ, to golden-haired Norse Sif. The earth goddess is usually depicted as a mother because the growth of plants and sustenance of animals come from her, mirroring the human experience of miraculously producing new life from the female body,* as well as nurturing and sustaining children, which historically has most often been women's work. (And, in fact, largely still is today: a 2016 study indicates that for every hour of childcare UK women do, men do twenty-four minutes.)

The 'mother' is one of the key elements in the 'triple goddess' concept that has been much debated by mythology scholars over the years. Triple goddesses

* It's weird that everyone goes on about Freud's theory of women all suffering from penis envy when a lot of mythology, and even current social anxiety about control of women's reproductive rights, seems more focused on male pregnancy envy: see the myths about Athena's and Aphrodite's births in this book for starters, the taboos around pregnant or menstruating women in many cultures, and the habit of dads-to-be saying, 'We're pregnant!'

– where three different personifications hang out within the same deity – appear in various mythologies including Norse, Ancient Greek and Celtic.

The division of human experience into three stages is, of course, not solely applied to women – the 'three ages of Man' (child, adult and OAP) are well known. And the triple goddess division of virgin, mother and crone

does roughly equate to familiar life phases for many women, tied to physical and menstrual transformations. But the triple goddess division sees female experience through a rather male gaze: virgin = shaggable; mother = shagged; crone = unshaggable.* People have always loved breaking women down into unflattering stereotypes centred around how they interact with or appear to them – the virgin/whore dichotomy being another well-known example (along with the girl-next-door/diva and the damsel-in-distress/ballbreaker). Never fear, we also get to be cat-lady spinsters, queen bees, career bitches, broken birds, mother hens (it's starting to feel like a zoo . . .), tarts with hearts, Mary Sues and final girls; the list goes on.

Alongside the creepy and outdated definitions in this list, some of these terms were invented to point out lazy and reductive representations of women on screen and in other media in order to change the way women are portrayed for the better. The Goddess movement (a neopagan group which arose in the 1970s to celebrate the divine feminine, in response to the male emphasis of most organised religions) has also purposefully looked to reclaim the triple goddess idea as a positive way of looking at female experience,

* See Amy Schumer's 'Last F**kable Day' sketch on YouTube for another NSFW angle on this.

embracing the terms 'crone' and 'hag' as definitions of wise older women. Most women today express combinations of any, all or none of the characteristics associated with these stereotypes, although still not always without censure. Your own complex personal balance of your values, attributes, skills and ambitions is what makes you unique; watch out for the ways in which our patriarchal society might try to fit you into one of the aforementioned boxes.

Coming back to the box labelled 'mothers': pre-birth control, having kids was a destiny that was pretty hard for women to avoid in culturally demanded heterosexual relationships. The move away from the assumption that motherhood is an essential feminine fate or experience has been liberating for everyone. The South American earth goddess Pachamama is an interesting example of a mother goddess who undercuts the idea that good motherhood is about giving your life over totally to your children. She was benevolent, nurturing and generous but also demanded good behaviour from her dependants (like those French women whose children don't throw food).* Pachamama was one of

* If you search for 'earth goddess' on Google Images you'll find a lot of pretty fan art showing Mother Earth as a smiling, peaceful woman with a dress made out of a wooded mountain and blossoming vines for hair. This might work for goddesses like Gaia, Pele and Pachamama but one of our favourite earth goddesses ain't quite so Instagrammable.

the prime deities of the Inca civilisation, which rose to prominence in the fifteenth century CE in Peru, although she is thought to have been worshipped in the Andean regions prior to this and still has devotees there today.

Where the idealised mother stereotype is supposed to keep giving with no requirement for a please or thank you, subsuming herself into the lives of her children, Pachamama is a strict goddess who insists on manners. When displeased, rather than call you by your full name and squeeze your hand a bit too tightly, she takes the form of an underground dragon and shakes up some earthquakes. Pachamama's children taught the first humans, formed by the creator god out of clay, how to survive in our world. Without her, agriculture fails, nature turns against us, people starve and die: she resists exploitation and requires regular offerings. No surprise that she has been embraced by climate-change activists and those seeking to protect the natural world from further disaster.

The Aztec goddess Tlaltecuhtli is described as a squatting monster with a huge open mouth full of flint teeth, further hungry mouths at her knees and elbows, clawed feet and hands and crocodile skin. She is constantly screaming for the blood of sacrificial victims. Her image often appeared in contact with the earth, away from human eyes, on the bottom of the special stoneware called eagle bowls, where the hearts of sacrificed humans were kept. Savage!

As the source of our food, Pachamama is a goddess of the harvest and her children include the life-giving sun himself, Inti (also sometimes her husband; don't sweat it, this happens a lot in myth); our favourite goddess of potatoes, Axomama; the more fashionable goddess of quinoa, Quinoamama; and the goddess of corn, Saramama. Her feast day is in August as this is considered the hardest time of year for her, when she needs the most attention from her adherents in order to get up the strength to provide new crops. Her followers used to sacrifice llamas and guinea pigs to her but nowadays they dress her shrines with petals and coca leaves, and make sure to spill the first sip of their beer onto the ground before drinking it as an offering to her. It has always been very important to keep Pachamama onside – right back when the Inca were establishing their magnificent capital, Cusco, they sacrificed a llama to her and entered the city holding its lungs blown-up like a gruesome party balloon, along with a gold disc representing Inti.

We don't have a solid written record about Pachamama, despite her prominence, because Inca mythology was transmitted orally and the narrative accounts we have were written down by Spanish invaders after the conquistador Pizarro conquered Cusco in 1533. So what can we learn from this long-enduring but mysterious mother goddess? The first lesson is that although it's great to see the Earth as feminine, it's important not to extrapolate damaging expectations of what women should be from this. Centuries of assuming that women are simple creatures (which is why so many of the goddesses in this book are associated with nature and instinct rather than culture or skills) mean that the labels used to describe us come from a limited selection. We all stereotype people, but we'd encourage you to strenuously resist patterns that have been dreamed up by men who like diminishing women. You are a complicated being and no stamp is going to satisfactorily define you, so decide your own balance and what your experience of womanhood will be. And look for that same balance in every area of your life; your recipe for happiness won't be the same as other people's, but bear in mind the time you spend on your health, your relationships, your work, your community and your inner life and purpose. That is how you build your own personal Pachamama-inspired ecosystem.

The other lesson we can learn from Pachamama is reciprocity. Don't just give, give, give but don't just take, take, take either. Neither course of action works out well. Equilibrium is what we're after. This extends to your family, your friends, your co-workers, your barista, your teacher, your doctor and the people you bump into in the street. It is a cliché universally acknowledged that you tend to get back out of life what you put in. But Pachamama doesn't give away her gifts for free. And finally, part of this reciprocity is due to Pachamama in her literal form as our planet: we all know we've exploited her resources too much – it's time to move the dial back to balance things out. Next time you're tempted to buy yourself a bottle of mineral water, think about Pachamama stretching herself out ready for an almighty earthquake, and find yourself a tap instead.

Mazu
and Keeping It Kind

CHINESE, CHINA

ALSO KNOWN AS

Heavenly Princess Who Protects the Nation and Shelters the People, of Marvellous Numen, Brilliant Resonance, Magnanimous Kindness, and Universal Salvation, Tianhou, Tianfe, Daughter of the Dragon, Empress of the Heavens

SKILLS

Weather Forecasting, Emitting Light, Guiding Ships, Calming Storms, Healing

RESPONSIBILITIES

The Sea, Sailors, Fishermen

It can often seem like the world is going down the pan. Every day we come across deliberate random acts of dickishness. That guy who watched with a sneer while you attempted to parallel-park for the seventeenth time. The trolls who joke about a celebrity's IQ level. The papers that fake-celebrate a post-partum pop star 'showcasing her new curves'. People can be extraordinarily unkind, in the most banal ways. But what if we turned that ship of sorrows right around, and endeavoured to respond to our own good fortune by carrying out acts of kindness for other people? Might the world not be a much, much better place? There's a growing move towards putting kindness and compassion at the heart of what we do – we see it enshrined in business philosophies, in growing trends of mindfulness, and as a backlash against toxic politics. Mazu, Chinese goddess of the sea, is the very embodiment of care and compassion.

Pleasingly, this great goddess originated from the deification of one extraordinary little girl. Born into a family of fishermen on Meizhou, a tiny island off the south-east coast of China, in 960 CE, Lin Mo showed otherworldly attributes from the off. Her birth was said to have been accompanied by bright lights and the heady scent of fresh blossom (which sounds much nicer than the blood-shit-screaming flavour of most deliveries). She was quiet and watchful, even as a tiny baby, and she had a photographic memory. Lin Mo began to study Buddhism at the age of ten and by the time she was a teenager was accepted by the people of her village as an exceptional healer.

One legend says that at the age of fifteen Lin Mo was with her gal pals checking out how their new dresses looked in the reflection of a pool when a creature burst out of the depths clutching a bronze disc. Her friends fled, but Lin Mo stood her ground and accepted the offering calmly, and from this point she really upped her godly game. Her skills were particularly suited to a community that was all about the sea. She could predict storms; she could appear as a bright light to guide boats in peril back to shore; and there are countless stories of her turning up in her trademark red to calm choppy waves. She was said to have set her own house on fire to act as a beacon guiding lost sailors home from sea.

Lin Mo's most famous – and tragic – legend tells of the attempted rescue of her father and brother from a typhoon. She was at home weaving when she fell into a trance, sensing her family was in trouble. Using her powers, she astrally projected herself out to their boat on the raging sea, and whipped her brother away from the treacherous waves and back onto land.

She was in the process of swimming home with her father clamped between her teeth, when her concerned mother shook her from her reverie at the loom. Lin Mo lost her grip and her father drowned. She searched for him for three desperate days before bringing his body home for a proper burial. Lin Mo channelled her terrible grief over her father's death into her spiritual work. At the heart of everything she did were care and compassion for the safety of all those around her, particularly fishermen.

Even her death had the air of the benevolent about it. At the age of twenty-eight she announced to her family that she had to leave to complete a journey alone. She climbed to the top of a nearby mountain, where she was shrouded in a thick mist, and to the soundtrack of soothing celestial music was carried heavenwards in a beam of light, leaving a rainbow behind her. Impressive! Almost immediately after her death she was deified as Mazu, goddess of the sea, by her townsfolk, and later imperial governments declared her a goddess as well – in fact she was promoted to grander and more extraordinary titles no fewer than thirty-six times.

As the maritime industry grew, so did worship of Mazu, spreading across the globe as Chinese emigrants travelled. The moniker of the port city of Macau came from Portuguese sailors mishearing her heavenly name. Today, she is worshipped by more than 200 million followers across China and South East Asia, where Mazu sculptures can be found in homes, cars and, of course, on boats. Many fisherman still light incense before a statue of her before heading out to sea – she gives them the confidence to go out and do a pretty dicey job.

One way to live a life with kindness at its heart is to start with yourself. We all make mistakes. We all mess up. The way forward lies in not wasting hours beating ourselves up for things that have gone wrong; our energy is so much better spent in picking ourselves up and learning from failure. It's hard to listen and constantly be caring to others, but it's worth it. A word of warning, though: women need to be wary about the repackaging of love, care and compassion. In the move towards celebrating the domestic and emotional space – which we're all for – we need to be aware that women have been trapped in the carer zone for centuries; it's part of a system of oppression built to keep us under the thumb. Someone needs to cook, clean and take care. And disproportionately, that someone is usually a woman. The division of domestic labour is gendered – and women do the bulk. According to a 2011 survey, fewer than 7 per cent of different-sex UK couples shared the burden equally, and even where a couple's jobs were equally challenging, the woman still did more housework. It's invisible work, unnoticed, unpaid, and it can lead to unhappiness in our relationships. We need to make sure that men and women navigate these turbulent seas together.

Mazu is a heroic and active example of looking after others. We're not suggesting you abandon all worldly possessions or set your house on fire, but we can make the world a better place by showing a bit more empathy and kindness towards our fellow humans. Buy a coffee for that person behind you in the queue, smile at people more, offer to carry that exhausted-looking person's bag up the stairs – hey, you could even leave a note on someone's car complimenting their awesome parallel-parking skills.

Tanit and the Art of Playing the Long Game

CARTHAGINIAN, NORTH AFRICA

ALSO KNOWN AS

Face of Baal, Tinith, Tinnit, Dea Caelestis (in Ancient Rome)

SKILLS

Protection, Dancing

RESPONSIBILITIES

Carthage, Fertility, The Moon, Rain, Women, Sex, Life, Ibiza

We live in a world where speed is prized and instant gratification is celebrated. We have fast food, instant messaging, speed dating, speed reading and even speed yoga, FFS! The answer to any question we may have, about anything, is only a click away. And while packing in all this supersonic experience, we feel we have less and less time to spend with our families and our friends. And when we are with them, we try to make it fast: ever edited sentences out of kids' bedtime stories to get them over and done with quicker? Or block-booked nights out with friends to kill two birds with one stone? Or done your washing up while you have a shower? On top of all this, the environmental implications of a fast and disposable society are clear to see.

It may seem strange to associate Ibiza – land of hedonism, partying and every type of instant gratification you could want to get your hands on – with the concept of patience and playing the long game, but bear with us, as one brilliant legend concerning Tanit, patron goddess of Ibiza, reveals just what rewards taking it slow can bring. Tanit was one of the Phoenicians' most important deities. She was originally the goddess of the great city of Carthage, which was founded on the north coast of what is now Tunisia in 814 BCE, giving them excellent trading access to the Mediterranean. The Phoenicians were seafaring imperial folk who originally came from Tyre (in modern-day Lebanon). Tanit is thought by many to have developed from the Middle Eastern star goddess, Ashtoreth (also known as Astarte), and her very

similar Mesopotamian version, Inanna (see pp. 30–7; also known as Ishtar).

Tanit was revered in Carthage as the mother of the gods. She was associated with the moon (her male counterpart, Baal Hammon, was the god of the sun – together they were the top couple of the Punic pantheon), as well as sex, dance (Ibiza!), fertility and the protection of women. She also had a rather less palatable penchant for child sacrifice. However, some scholars believe that mass children's graves at important sites of Tanit worship were in fact more likely those of premature or stillborn babies that did not survive the ravages of ancient childbirth, handed to the goddess for safe passage into the afterlife.

Tanit came late to the Phoenician party, only appearing as Baal Hammon's consort in the fifth century BCE, but there was no need for her to rush, because it is clear she soon outshone her golden boyfriend in the popularity stakes. She appears on countless fragments of pottery, coins and jewellery, and even managed to nab her own symbol: a triangle with a line and circle,* which sounds underwhelming but is actually pretty extraordinary – no other Carthaginian deity was enough of a superbrand to achieve their own logo. She

*  It looks a bit like a drawing of a woman in a dress or a rearranged Deathly Hallows sign.

was exported beyond Carthage as the Phoenicians extended their empire, and when a port was established in Ibiza in 654 BCE, Tanit came too. The story goes that as the Phoenicians landed on the island a storm whipped up dust, which made the rivers flow red – they took this as a sign they should establish a cult for their favourite goddess there.

Tanit has real staying power, and millions of those who visit Ibiza for its spiritual vibe still see her today as protectress of Ibiza and especially its women. One story in particular shows the benefits of playing the long game her way. Historically, Ibizan tradition decreed that the very best fertile farmland in the interior of the island was inherited – surprise, surprise – by the men and boys of a family, whereas the women were left with coastal areas, bleached by sun, rendered useless (in agricultural terms) by the salt of the sea. In the 1960s, the women of the island, fully fed up with the economic trap that meant their only way to escape poverty was to marry a farmer, gathered under a full moon to dance and pray to Tanit. Not long after this night-time ritual the hippies arrived, which perhaps wasn't quite the gift they hoped for, but these visitors soon spread the word about the infinite joys of the white isle, and soon after that tourism really took off. That dry, arid, infertile coast was where it was at: the economic pendulum swung in favour of *las mujeres*.

It's pretty impressive that a goddess whose first possible incarnation (as Inanna, don't sweat it) was worshipped six thousand years ago is still honoured today at the Cova des Culleram in San Vicente, in the peaceful north of the island. Thousands of people visit these caves every year – where a shrine filled with six hundred terracotta statues of Tanit was discovered in 1907 – to offer her prayers and gifts. Countless hotels, shops and bars are also named after her and statues and idols of her keep watch over homes and nightclubs across the island. And isn't it a joy that the moon goddess still presides over the island of full-moon dance parties?

The short game is easy, fun and delivers instant benefits and pleasure. Why save that extra tenner when you could spend it? Why bother preparing for that presentation when you know half the people in the room won't be listening? Just watch one more episode – that extra hour away from bed won't make *that* much of a difference. But the costs of short-termism accumulate – those hours missed staying up late, those pennies frittered away do end up making a big difference. So here are our simple strategies for investing in the future: prepare for that meeting properly rather than making some bullshit up on the spot, spend less and save more, finish that maths assignment before you gad about. We have too many choices and not enough time to make them, and that can feel overwhelming. Tanit's everlasting reputation and relevance for the women and partygoers of Ibiza show us just how valuable playing the long game can be, Tanit-style.

Kali and Bringing It

HINDU, INDIA

ALSO KNOWN AS

She Who Is Black, She Who Is Death, Kaushika (the Sheath), Kali-Ma (Mother Kali)

SKILLS

Dancing, Fighting Evil, Demon-Disposal, Saving the World

RESPONSIBILITIES

Death, Time, Doomsday, Female Sexuality, Violence, Regeneration

Tune into any radio phone-in or TV debate, read countless threads on social media, and it soon becomes apparent that there's a whole lot of bile and venom out there. Even the sat-nav seems to have a right grump on. But we also know that, as long as we don't let it stagnate and turn ugly, anger can bring about positive change. Martin Luther King wrote that the 'supreme task is to organise and unite people so that their anger becomes a transforming force', and in our personal lives, too, it's important to recognise the power of strong emotions to push us into action.

Kali is the goddess of death, time, doomsday, female sexuality and violence. But she is also symbolic of mother love, in all its ferocity and complexity. Kali nurtures *and* destroys, encapsulating the idea that life cannot exist without death. Millions of Hindus worship her today in the form of Mother Kali. She is often depicted in her magnificent trademark victory pose – astride her supine consort, the great god Shiva, mouth agape in a wide smile, bloody tongue lolling out, bedecked with a necklace of skulls and a skirt made of severed human arms, wild hair tumbling down the blue or black of her back. Oh, and she's usually holding aloft a severed human head. As a symbol of female strength, she's pretty memorable.

The richly complex pantheon of Hindu gods and

goddesses has been with us for thousands of years, first appearing in the songs of the *Rig Veda* at about the same time as the Ancient Egyptians and the Mesopotamians were doing their thing. The *Rig Veda*, believed to have been composed around 1200 BCE, comprises over a thousand poems grouped into mandalas, or circles – and is one of the world's oldest religious texts. A triumvirate of gods is central to it, responsible for the creation, upkeep and destruction of the world. Brahma is the creator, and most Hindu gods and goddesses represent some side of him. He's in charge of space and time, and he recreates the world every *kalpa*, which for him is a day and a night, but for humans a rather more punchy thousands of millions of years. Vishnu is the protector of the world and his role is to appear in times of trauma to chill everything out. Shiva is the destroyer – he obliterates in order to recreate, making the world more perfect each time – and he vacillates between extremes. Sometimes he's all about abstinence; sometime he's a hedonist, dancing wildly; and it's his benign and super-relaxed wife Parvati who brings him balance.

However, even pink and fluffy Elle Woods has a steely core and Kali is Parvati's dark side. She has various creation stories, each with a delicious thread of violence and intensity. In one story the gods were being harassed by the demon Daruka, who could only be killed by a woman. Parvati jumped down Shiva's throat to collect poison to deal with Daruka and burst out of him as a rampaging Kali, who defeated the demon. In another, humans and gods alike were being harassed by the demon Raktabija (blood-seed), who had the endlessly frustrating ability to replicate himself each time a drop of his blood was shed. The gods pooled their *shakti* (divine energy) together to make a supergoddess capable of dispatching Raktabija. Kali was the result. She set about her task with relish, swallowing his clones whole so that no drops could fall and then decapitating Raktabija and chugging down all his blood. Another birth story has the warrior goddess Durga in battle with Mahisha, the buffalo demon, who again could only be bumped off by a woman. Durga became so furious during the fight that her anger coalesced in her forehead like the mother of all headaches and finally burst out in the form of Kali, who went wild and ate Mahisha and his entire army, stringing a nice necklace out of their skulls as she went.

But Kali's righteous indignation has to be tempered with calm, and often there is a moment when the extremity of her feelings must be balanced. When her bloodthirsty dancing threatens to go out of control, Shiva lies down in front of her to jolt her out of the single-mindedness of her fury. In some accounts he appears as a baby in order to activate her maternal instinct and divert her from her apocalyptic path. Sometimes we all need a time-out. But Kali's temper is a force of propulsion and decisiveness: her astonishingly effective action would be impossible without it – she arrives in these tales when there is no hope left and terrible force must be met with, um, terrible force.

Kali is a goddess who encompasses opposites – a demon-killer and a gentle mother; terrifying and benevolent; death and life – and she shows that by accepting contrary and unpredictable forces, we can be liberated from worrying about them. Different groups within Hinduism focus on different aspects of her qualities and stories, and her fame has spread far beyond Asia. Her image is incredibly powerful and is recognised worldwide. When they first came across her, Christian colonists in India were both horrified and fascinated, exoticising her and focusing on her sexual aspects. She has been portrayed in various different ways in the West, which are often offensively far from her transcendent origins: from being heralded as a heroic symbol of female sexual liberation and power by some feminist groups and New Age believers, to being depicted as the centre of a bloodthirsty evil demon cult in *Indiana Jones and the Temple of Doom* (which is ironic, considering Kali's personal history with demons). Mick Jagger apparently was inspired by Kali for the Rolling Stones' famous hot lips logo.

Kali shows us how to channel outrage into a force for good. She is an outsider, a motivator and a disruptor and she often encourages Shiva into disruptive behaviour too. She is always in motion, just like time keeps ticking along. When you really care about something you want to take urgent action; it makes your heart beat faster and starts your adrenaline pumping, taking you to a place where you feel truly alive. This is the kind of powerful energy that can move mountains. Make sure you use it when you feel it and dance your way to victory, just like Kali.

Sedna
and Prioritising Self-Care

INUIT, NORTH AMERICA
AND GREENLAND

ALSO KNOWN AS

One-Who-Never-Wanted-to-Marry, Sanna, Sea Mother, Queen of Adlivun, Arnakuagsak (old woman from the sea), Arnapkapfaaluk (big bad woman), Nuliayuk (old food dish)

SKILLS

Marine Animal Management, Judgement, Weather Manipulation

RESPONSIBILITIES

Sea Mammals, Fish Stocks, The Underworld, Monitoring Human Behaviour

We all have bad-hair days, dark days or one of those days when there's no milk, the bus is late, your socks are wet, you smear mascara down your top, your phone battery dies, your best friend's boyfriend dumps her, the printer runs out

of paper, and everyone has forgotten it's your birthday. Days when you feel overwhelmed, when you long to burrow back under the duvet and stay there. But we try to just keep trucking on. These are the hardest moments to remember to take a moment for ourselves.

The story of the Inuit sea spirit, Sedna, shows the tricky balancing act required between looking after those around you and looking after yourself. And how the two things are actually dependent on each other: self-care is not the same as being selfish. Sedna is the most prominent deity in the myths of the coastal Inuit peoples who live in the Arctic regions of Canada, Alaska and Greenland. There are several different versions of her origin story but all of them explain how she came to be the potent figure known as the Sea Mother.

The ancestors of today's Inuit population are thought to have crossed over to Greenland and North America from Asia over fifteen thousand years ago, when lower sea levels meant there was a land route available across what is now the fifty-mile stretch of water between Russia and Alaska known as the Bering Strait. Before sustained European contact began in the sixteenth and seventeenth centuries – bringing traders and drunken whalers, followed by invasive diseases and missionaries – the Inuit way of life was focused on self-sufficient, close-knit communities. Living in freezing conditions that most of us cushy, centrally-heated sofa-dwellers would not have the skills to survive even if swathed in Thinsulate, many coastal Inuit lived a semi-nomadic lifestyle sustained by hunting and fishing and the priorities of very distinct seasons. The lack of plant life in their territory for much of the year meant that agriculture was impossible, but the sea provided almost everything that Inuit families needed: food (narwhal and whale skin are actually great sources of vitamin C – who knew?); fur, skin and bones for equipment, clothing and housing; and oil for fuel.

Inuit mythology varies by region, and was told orally before Europeans started to make written accounts in the nineteenth century. The stories tend to involve a very close link between the people and the land and all it provides. Traditional Inuit religion has animist elements: hunters have great respect for the creatures they rely on for food. Animism sees no separation between the physical and spiritual worlds and holds that all natural phenomena – humans, animals, rivers, plants – have a spiritual element or soul. In the past Inuit hunters carried out specific rituals to show respect when an animal was hunted; ignoring these was taboo and considered likely to bring misfortune to the group. The people who looked after these codes of behaviour and worked out how to fix problems were the *angakkuit,* or shamans, who could communicate with non-human aspects of nature. Groups who broke taboos – with disrespectful sub-par hunting techniques, for example – were punished by the sea goddess Sedna, who would cause bad weather and keep seals and whales down deep in her undersea kingdom, refusing to let them provide dinner. Without the intercession of a skilled *angakkuq* to soothe the Sea Mother, the villagers starved.

The story of how Sedna netted her watery domain begins with her as an ordinary girl. She starts her path to becoming extraordinary simply because she didn't want to get married. This might seem like small fry to us but having in-laws to rely on and a family unit to support you is rather more critical in a world where the weather and natural resources are unpredictable, and the bonds of kinship are crucial to helping people work together. Sedna's father was deeply unimpressed by her wish to stay young, free and single. In one version of her story she infuriates him by refusing human suitors and marrying a dog instead. She gives birth to puppies before her father kills her dog-husband. She then sends her pups away and they become the ancestors of different 'races', including dwarves, giants and Europeans, making her the mother of all peoples.

In other stories, Sedna is kidnapped or forced by her father to marry a seabird (a fulmar or petrel usually, if you're after specifics). Even in the stories where she falls for the bird willingly, she changes her mind when she gets back to his nest and is grossed out by how dirty and unpleasant her new domestic situation is. When her father comes to visit she asks him to take her home. However, on the boat journey back her furious and jilted bird-husband whips up a huge storm and Sedna's father hastily knocks her overboard in the hope of calming the raging bird's wrath. Sedna clings on to the boat and won't let go. Trigger warning: this is where we get to the brutal bit of the story.

Sedna's father is so desperate to get rid of her at this point that he starts cutting off her fingers to make her let go of his boat. As her severed digits fall into the sea they become seals, walruses, whales and polar bears. Sedna sinks down to the bottom of the ocean. Deep in the icy depths, she ends up ruling over sea creatures as a 'Mistress of Beasts'* and 'crone' figure. She also governs the frozen underworld known as Adlivun, a kind of limbo where the spirits of the dead go

* See Epona on pp. 171–9 for more about goddesses and their animal pals. The Canadian and Alaskan Haida volcano goddess Dzelarhons is another Mistress of Beasts figure who had a bad marriage and went on to protect animals and fish.

before they ascend to the moon to live happily before reincarnation.

Because of her attachment to marine mammals, Sedna is often depicted with a whale's tail in the beautiful carvings that are still made of her. Parts of her story call to mind what we know about mermaids, although not the smiley, glittery-shell-bra kind. Mermaids in older legends are usually seen as sinister and dangerous threats to sailors and fishermen and Sedna is certainly dangerous when displeased. By trapping the seals and other animals in her kingdom she denies people their source of sustenance, with disastrous consequences. Mermaids are also often depicted combing their hair, which echoes another part of Sedna's story.

When her people fail to keep to the customs and laws of their society, which govern everything from relationships to the correct rituals around hunting and eating, Sedna finds her hair becoming tangled and infested with parasites that represent these broken rules. Because she has no fingers she cannot comb out her hair herself and so becomes increasingly enraged. It takes a brave *angakkuq* to solve this situation by going into a trance which allows him to visit the goddess in her undersea realm, where she lives with her repentant father and her dog and, in some accounts, her girlfriend, Qailertetang. Here the *angakkuq* has to pass through various dangers including an ice abyss and a cauldron of boiling seals before he can reach Sedna's whalebone house and patiently comb and braid her hair. On returning from his trance he can let the village know exactly what has put her nose out of joint, and once this is sorted the seals and whales return to their waters.

Sedna's story is thought-provoking on many levels. We are all part of groups with their own rules: this might be your own close family's ways of doing things, or those of your peer group or society as a whole. Sedna went against the expectations of her community by refusing to marry. Her story demonstrates the tension between wanting to act for your own benefit and for the benefit of others (we're sure that in the cold light of day her dad didn't feel too great about trying to chuck his daughter overboard to save his own skin). Altruism and having community spirit are both important but this doesn't mean you have to always follow the herd. For example, many British cultural norms have in the past been hugely damaging to minority groups and the less advantaged: should women be banned from pubs without a male companion? Should black people have less access to housing than white people? Should women be paid less than men for the same work? Should people in wheelchairs just have to deal with the fact that the world is full of steps? It seems incredible that only a few decades ago the acceptable answer to all these questions was 'yes'. It's crucial to interrogate the rules you come up against and decide for yourself whether they are good for you and good for others or not.

The other thing to note in Sedna's story is that she had a really bad day, and it all worked out OK in the end. She lost something (or some things, her fingers) and one door closed (on living a human life and combing her own hair), but at the same time she gained something (a kingdom) and a window opened (on power). Sedna gives a lot, by providing people with food, but she does retreat from the world and take time for herself when things get too much. When you next feel stormy or snowed under, make sure you communicate how you're feeling to someone. It's only by looking after each other and letting people know we need a hand that we can untangle our messes and get things back in order. Even on the very worst bad-hair day imaginable, Sedna's still not too proud to accept help from others.

The Selkie Wife

and Saying No

SCOTTISH, SCOTLAND

ALSO KNOWN AS

Silkie, Kópakonan (Faroe Islands), Haaf-Fish (Shetland), Marmennlar (Iceland)

SKILLS

Swimming, Naked Sunbathing, Domestic Management, Singing

RESPONSIBILITIES

Family, Freedom

It's just two letters. One itsy-bitsy little syllable. But how can such a tiny word be so powerful and so bloody difficult to say? 'No' is a definitive term from the word go: it's one of the first words humans learn, and it's what our parents say to us as children when we make unreasonable demands about attending school in our leopard onesies, or ask for an actual real live bear for Christmas. But it's also one of the key things we're taught *not* to say from a very young age, especially if we have been brought up as girls. Girls are conditioned to be compliant, to be considerate of others' feelings; we're taught that saying no is rude. This is why a lot of women find it hard to say no in later life, and why you can find yourself agreeing to all sorts of mad shit simply because you're avoiding answering in the negative (laser-tag hen do in the outer Hebrides, anyone?).

The discomfort we feel when we have to refuse something usually comes from a good place – we don't want to deliver rejection, we don't want to appear aggressive or uncaring. But much as we support the life-enhancing power of 'yes', there are limits. And yes, we can unlearn this socially powered mechanism and stop subjugating our own needs to those of others. Yes, we can harness the moxie of this small but mighty word! Yes, we can use it as our very own superpower! The selkies of Orkney can show us how.

Selkies are extraordinary shapeshifting characters from Scottish mythology, closely related to merfolk, who also appear in the folklore of Ireland, Scandinavia, Iceland and the Faroes. 'Selkie' is the word for 'seal' on Orkney. These seal-people live in the sea for most of the year, but are sometimes able to shed their skins and assume human form. It is in this guise that they – both male and female – have the ability to drive even indifferent men and women wild with lust. You may not ever have looked at a seal and thought they were superhot (although they do have nice eyes), but their bipedal incarnations are winning them Sexiest Mythological Creature of the Year awards time after time. There are many hundreds of stories about them handed down through oral tradition. The Orkney folklorist Walter Traill Dennison recorded one such tale, 'The Goodman of Wastness', in the late nineteenth century.

The Goodman of Wastness was a good-looking, brawny and prosperous young farmer, an Orcadian Richard Madden, if you will. The local lassies took a shine to him, but he turned them all down, gaining an iffy reputation for committing the unpardonable sin of celibacy. He was unrepentant, believing women brought more trouble than they were worth, and were sent only to mither men. 'If yin owld fool Adam hidd-no been bewitched be his wife, he might still be in the Gardeen o'Eden the day.' (Rough translation: Stupid Adam; all Eve's fault.)

One day, the Goodman was walking along the beach when he spotted some selkie people playing naked on a rock, having dispensed with their sealskin duds in order to enjoy a bit of nudist beach fun. He sneaked up on them and managed to grab one sea nymph's sealskin before she was able to escape back to the sea. With the skin tucked under his arm, the Goodman made his way back across the shore, until he heard sobbing behind him. It was the selkie woman whose skin he had taken, weeping and begging to get it back. Without it, she couldn't return to her selkie husband or the rest of her family. 'I cinno live in da sea withoot it. I cinno bide amung me ain folk waythoot me selkie-skin.'

Disturbingly, the sight of a greetin', skuddy (weeping and naked) woman begging him for mercy seemed to do just the trick for the previously stone-hearted Goodman, and he fell passionately in love with her on the spot. Men can be gross about vulnerable women.*

The Goodman eventually managed to persuade the selkie to agree to come and live with him as his wife – though in reality this is less persuasion and more coercion: she has no choice because she can't go back to the sea without her skin and he absolutely refuses to give it to her. The Selkie Wife turns out to be great at land-lubbing domesticity; she is beautiful, thrifty and kind, and she bears him seven children – four boys and three girls, the bonniest bairns in all the isles. From the outside, theirs is a perfect life, but the Selkie Wife carries a great sadness with her. She is often to be found gazing searchingly at the sea, and sometimes sings a song so haunting that animals stop feeding and children pause their play to stand as still as statues. Anyone defined and valued only by how great they are at household chores might reasonably feel like this, irrespective of the whole forced-marriage piece.

One day, the Goodman went fishing with his four boys. The two older girls were on the beach gathering

* No, we don't mean *all* men. We mean *some* men, *some* of the time. Enough to notice.

limpets, but the littlest daughter stayed at home with a sore foot. With the house all but empty, the Selkie Wife began – as she always did when she found herself alone – to search for her sealskin. Her daughter asked her what she was looking for, and her mother replied that she was searching for a beautiful sealskin that would help heal her injured foot. The daughter knew exactly where it was and showed her. With a huge whoop of joy the Selkie Wife rushed to the shore and flung on her skin, shifting to selkie form. She swam through the waves to where her selkie husband was waiting for her, calling to the Goodman as he spotted her from his boat, 'Farewell tae thee. I liked thee weel enough fur too war geud tae me, bit I love better me man o'the sea.' ('Bye bye. I *quite* liked you – but I much prefer my selkie husband.') The family never saw the Selkie Wife again.

The therianthropic,* thalassic** tale of the Selkie Wife can teach us a lot about the power of saying no. She's coerced into a life that puts her own needs right at the bottom of the pile. On the surface, hers is a happy,

* A swank word to work into conversation as often as possible. It means 'part animal, part human', from the Ancient Greek words *therion* ('beast') and *anthropos* ('human'). Bastet, with her cat's head, on pp. 46–52, is therianthropic.

** Means 'of the sea', from the Greek *thalassa* ('sea'). We're just showing off now.

abundant family, but in fact it's a toxic marriage built on her subjugation. The selkie knows she can only be happy and her true self in the wild sea, so when the opportunity arises to say no to her gilded cage, she grabs it. She says no to her husband, home and children – it's a profoundly empowering act.

So if constantly saying yes is leading you to stress and anxiety, you need to find a comfortable way to say no. Don't apologise while doing it: say it fast instead and say it true. We often shit-sandwich our 'no's when we shouldn't, so instead of saying, 'You are such a great friend, I'd love to pick your car up from the airport for you, but I've actually got plans that day, but if it's really important to you of course I'll find a way!' try being direct: 'I can't, I'm afraid, as I'm busy.' 'Not this time' is a useful phrase when it comes to politely declining invitations. When you're mustering up the courage to let someone down, be sure to visualise the benefit your refusal is going to give to pep you up: so when you're excusing yourself from your boss's birthday party, fully imagine how great it's going to feel to be curled up in your pjs watching Netflix instead.

We all have our own priorities: for the Selkie Wife it was her first husband and family. Decide your true feelings about what's being asked of you, and respond accordingly. By learning how to say no, you're in fact saying yes to yourself. Say yes to the things that make *you* happy. Don't go on that third date with awful Paul from Marketing just because you know he'll be hurt if you knock it on the head; head off to that pop-up to drink a Grapefruit Basil Mimosa with your buddies instead. Don't agree to collect your boss's kids' birthday presents; spend your lunch hour getting down to the next chapter of that brilliant book you're so gripped by. Use 'no' as your very own selkie-skin, as armour to protect you from people out to take advantage, and as a weapon to set you swimming free.

The Wawilak Sisters

and Building Resilience

YOLNGU, AUSTRALIA

ALSO KNOWN AS

The Wawalag Sisters, The Wagilag Sisters

SKILLS

Nomenclature, Dancing, Defining Landscape, Establishing Rituals

RESPONSIBILITIES

Initiation, Fertility

Apart from perhaps those perfectly filtered Insta-influencers who appear to enjoy charmed lives of constant glamour, affection and fulfilment (perhaps the most skilful myth-weavers of our times), no one gets away with a life of complete plain sailing. When the ground seems unsteady beneath your feet and you're in need of resilience, the story of the Wawilak Sisters is an inspiring one.

One of the oldest continuous cultures on earth is that of the Australian Aboriginal peoples. There is evidence that humans were living in Australia 65,000 years ago. They are believed to have migrated there by sea from Asia in the earliest known instance of seafaring. Rising sea levels then isolated the continent until much, much later, when trade with the people of Papua New Guinea and Indonesia began, before the arrival of the Europeans in the seventeenth century.

As with so many of the other cultures in this book, the sight of European boats pulling up to the coast definitely did not mark a good day for the approximately one million inhabitants of Australia. At this time Australian Aboriginal peoples thrived across the mighty continent and amongst its gloriously diverse ecosystems in hundreds of distinct groups defined primarily by kinship bonds, speaking hundreds of different languages. The complex society and mythology of their communities were vastly different in philosophy and organisation to that of the predominantly British invaders and it remains difficult for outsiders to properly appreciate all their aspects.

Many of the first British scholars to record Aboriginal histories, customs and myths misunderstood a great deal and brought their own world view to the party. They were also often told only the 'kids' version' of sacred myths, as the knowledge of many stories is only accessible to specific people even within the Aboriginal communities. Crucially, they failed to appreciate the deep connection between Aboriginal communities and their land, assuming that because many groups were semi-nomadic, they could be easily moved on to make way for the British settlers keen to find their fortunes in this new colony.

The theft of territory and transgression of sacred places that followed led to conflict between the Aboriginal and coloniser communities, which along with the influx of European diseases decimated the population, which dipped to just over a hundred thousand by 1901. It was widely believed by the colonial government that the Aboriginal population would conveniently disappear entirely, but the community proved way more resilient than they imagined. Today the Aboriginal population of Australia is around

745,000, making up 3.1 per cent of the overall population. They are still subject to discrimination, the after-effects of the brutal appropriation of their land and the assimilationist policies that saw children taken from their families right up to the 1970s. Shockingly, it was only in 1992 that the law was changed to recognise that Australia was their country at the moment the British first arrived and claimed it.

Aboriginal mythology is centred around the idea of the Dreaming. This refers to the mythic past when the continent and its inhabitants were formed, but also incorporates the spiritual dimension of the present and future. The distinct communities mean that regional stories about the Dreaming are varied, although they sometimes connect with and reflect one another. In the Dreaming, Australia is populated by supernatural ancestral beings who through their actions establish the topography and the laws and customs of the people. Amazingly, many of the stories refer accurately to far-distant geological changes that scientists have since verified, such as volcanic explosions and changing sea levels and flora. One set of researchers have investigated over twenty stories from across the continent that appear to accurately describe a 120m rise in sea level that took place between eighteen thousand and seven thousand years ago.

One of the most influential myths from the northern coastal region called Arnhem Land is that of the ancestral beings known as the Wawilak Sisters. Arnhem Land is home to a vibrant majority community of the Yolngu people. The story of the sisters is told in various different ways, often dramatised through ritual, dance, oral storytelling and artistic works. It's a rich narrative that is thought-provoking on many levels, but its true meaning can only be interpreted by the initiated community it is intended for: our take here can only ever be that of outsiders. Even the term 'the Dreaming' is an interpretation of words from many different Australian Aboriginal languages which was established by Europeans in the nineteenth century and is considered by many to be misleading.

The Wawilak Sisters journey across the landscape at the time of creation. As they travel they generously give names to the animals and plants, like the bandicoots, yams and opossums, and indicate whether they will become sacred or not in future. The older sister is pregnant by someone within her kinship group and, when it's time, her sister helps her give birth to a son near to a waterhole. However, when the sisters try to make a well-earned dinner by cooking the animals they've caught, the uncooperative critters jump up, run away and throw themselves into the waterhole. Things get worse when some of the new mother's post-partum blood runs into the waterhole, waking the great Rainbow Serpent Yurlunggur, who lives there. Yurlunggur emerges, bringing lightning, storms and floods.

Despite their distraction techniques, including dancing and singing, and their efforts to take shelter in a hut they build, Yurlunggur eats the sisters and the baby. However, he is shamed by other snakes into regurgitating them because the sisters are actually from his own kinship group and so should not be treated as snacks. His efforts to throw them back up by thrashing about create a sacred ceremonial dancing place in the landscape. The sisters are revived by biting ants. The good times don't last for long as Yurlunggur swallows them again, and from this point on he speaks with their voices and doles out their wisdom, in a neat trick of ventriloquism. After this the sisters come to the men of the region in dreams and teach them the rituals they need to carry out.

Snakes are some of the hottest characters in world mythology. The Jim Broadbents of the mythological world, they are never out of work and are always popping up in vastly disparate places, either as phallic fertility totems, chaotic dragons or personifications of evil or rebirth. In the form of the rainbow, linking the earth to the sky, bringing nourishing rain and illustrating the circular nature of life and death with their shape, the serpent is a universal ancestral being, recognised across Australian Aboriginal cultures. Yurlunggur has many different names, appearing sometimes as female, sometimes male, and sometimes with no gender, but usually as a force that is both creative and destructive. In the story of the sisters he can be interpreted as both a masculine attack on the women and, in a more positive way, as a womb swallowing them ready for their rebirth.

It's interesting in this story that the culture heroes are female and that as well as enacting the primal Mother-Earthy business of childbirth they are responsible for the civilising act of defining the universe by naming and setting distinctions between living things and creating religious ceremonies. The knowledge of what is sacred and what is taboo, and who is and isn't kin, are key organising principles in many Aboriginal communities. For example, for the Yolngu it's crucial that people marry outside their kinship group, and in some versions of this story the birth of the older sister's child marks the establishment of the system whereby children are automatically from the opposite kinship group to their mother. In some accounts, Yurlunggur's anxiety about eating his own kin leads him to penitently regurgitate the sisters (don't get out the 'Welcome Home!' banners just yet; they then turn to stone), but not the child, as he doesn't belong to the same group.

This story also explains why in the Yolngu and other Australian Aboriginal groups men have control over certain religious knowledge and many religious ceremonies. In many other places around the world, from South America to Papua New Guinea, there are myths which propose that power used to reside with women but, because of a mistake the women made, ended up with men. The Mesopotamian story of the great female sea dragon Tiamat, who was stabbed to death by the warrior Marduk, is the most famous and has been interpreted by some to illustrate a general movement over time from the dominance of terrestrial goddesses to sky gods, such as those that prevail in organised religions today.

The rituals that sprang from the Wawilak Sisters' myth are to do with the rite-of-passage initiations of boys into manhood, which are kept completely secret from women. Male initiation rites like these are often interpreted as being about ritually enacting death so that there can be rebirth into a new adult life, and about marking the separation of boys from their mothers to join them in solidarity with other men. In these rituals the initiates and other men spill their own blood to reflect the experience of the sisters and dramatise key moments from the story. Across many cultures, initiation ceremonies require endurance: pain is a natural part of life and must be confronted in order to properly engage with the adult world to the full.

In some versions of the story it is the sisters' menstrual blood, rather than afterbirth, that aggravates the snake, but in both cases it is something biologically female which is associated with their generative power and which sets off the action. Childbirth and the menstrual cycle* have often been seen to connect women to the seasons and other natural phenomena like the waxing and waning of the moon, and to creation and death: all powerful natural forces. Blood is both sacred and taboo in many different cultures; in some, women keep separate from the rest of their groups while menstruating and have limits on their behaviour, particularly around sex and food. (The part of

* Human periods are actually quite interesting. And not just because of all that rollerblading and volleyball-playing that tampon companies insist goes on when the painters are in. Only a few other animals menstruate – some primates and bats and, weirdly, the elephant shrew – and not many seem to get the menopause, some whales being a notable exception. Other mammals only create a cushy womb lining for a potential baby once that baby is on the way. One theory for why the majority of XX-women regularly build up womb lining and then expel it if it's not needed is that human embryos enmesh themselves so assertively into the womb that there needs to already be tissue there to protect the mother from its offspring's demands – babies are very efficient parasites.

the Wawilak Sisters' story where the animals jump up from the cooking fire links to this, as it's cooking that gets rid of the bloodiness of meat.)

So how do the Wawilak Sisters teach us about resilience when it seems their story is about their power being eclipsed? One way of reading this myth is that the sisters live on in the most important, spiritual, plane, and are constantly brought to life by the languages and rituals they instigated. In this way they survive being eaten (and vommed up and eaten again) and become part of the great Rainbow Serpent, which also represents cyclical time. They do not have an easy time of it, to be sure, but in their fate is an acceptance that difficult things happen and change is inevitable. They are swallowed by their troubles but not entirely bumped off by them – their contribution and significance is still celebrated today. So let their story get your blood up, and remember: life is tough, and so are you.

Rangda
and Enjoying Single Life

BALINESE, BALI

ALSO KNOWN AS

Calon Arang, Queen of Death,
Queen of the Leyaks

SKILLS

Sorcery, Dancing, Eating Kids,
Organising Plagues

RESPONSIBILITIES

Dancing for Eternity, Keeping Balance

You know the story. Their eyes meet-cute across a crowded room. They fall madly in love. They're cruelly parted. They find each other again and live happily ever after.

It's a familiar trope employed by narrative-makers over millennia as the dream scenario, and it heavily influences the way our society views single people and, needless to say, single women in particular. As long as happiness and romantic love are seen as perfect bedfellows, we'll keep being defined by whether we have a partner or not. There is huge pressure on women to settle down, get married and have babies – it's all around us. (And no, it's not just your Uncle Nev cracking the 'always the bridesmaid' joke and making that tick-tock noise. At every. Wedding. You. Have. Ever. Been. To.) A quick glance at the glossies shows us how pernicious couple propaganda is: 'Ten Things to Get Guys to Notice You', 'Why Guys Pull Away (and What to Do When It Happens)', 'What Makes a Man Want to Marry' – these are real examples of contemporary magazine headlines, we're sorry to say. Everywhere you turn, the idea of going solo is portrayed in an astonishingly negative light, when in reality recent research suggests that single, childless women are happier than their sprogged-up peers. Marriage rates are dropping and singledom is on the

rise. The fabulously fierce witch goddess Rangda offers a salutary tale about the art of embracing alone time.

On the Indonesian island of Bali, Rangda is a significant player in Balinese Hindu mythology, in which no demon or god is entirely good or bad. Rangda is the female embodiment of divine negative energy, locked in an eternal struggle with her counterpart Barong, the (male, naturally) embodiment of more positive attributes. Barong resembles a lion with a magnificent lush flowing mane, whereas Rangda is terrifyingly uncute, with long shaggy hair, black-and-white striped body, fangs dripping crimson blood, huge bulging eyes and a metre-long bright red tongue flapping to the floor – reminiscent of the Hindu goddess Kali, with whom she is associated. Consecrated masks of each character are usually kept in village temples, and are used when this duo's most famous story is acted out in regular festivities. But Balinese mythology is not as straightforward as Rangda = good, Barong = bad; Rangda's extraordinary powers can in fact heal, and ol' goody-two-shoes Barong's are always susceptible to misuse.

Rangda started out as a fearsome widow called Calon Arang (Rangda's name is derived from the Old Javanese word for 'widow'), who was a powerful witch. Calon Arang had a beautiful daughter called

Ratna, who, despite her gorgeousness, couldn't find a husband in her village because everyone was so shit-scared of her admittedly worrisome mum. Calon Arang was enraged with her neighbours about the treatment of her daughter so she sacrificed a local girl to the goddess Durga,* who then delivered a flood which killed half of the villagers. The king's advisor sent a man called Mpu Bahula to sort this mayhem out by marrying Calon Arang's daughter in a magnificent ceremony that lasted seven days and seven nights. Mpu Bahula had heard about the magical book that Calon Arang used to cast her spells, and while she was sleeping off the epic seven-night party, he stole it and gave it to his boss. Calon Arang was furious and kicked off at the king's advisor about it, but without the power of her spellbook she lost the ensuing battle, and the village was finally safe from her.

Another story casts Rangda as the queen of the *leyaks* (black-magic spirits who feast on humans and especially like to go after pregnant women – nice!). In this tale she was originally a Javanese princess whose hobby was a bit of sorcery. When she was widowed, her sons ostracised her and sent her to live in the jungle. Rangda took terrible revenge on their kingdom

* Durga is a stunning, golden, lion-riding, ten-armed Hindu warrior goddess, closely associated with the wilder demon-slaying goddess Kali.

by gathering all the *leyaks*, who wrought havoc via pestilence, plague and all-round bad times. After she defeated the soldiers her sons sent to deal with her, and went about using their entrails as fashion accessories, her boys called on good old Barong. Barong and Rangda's subsequent duel is represented in the dances that many tourists in Bali love to watch, which are performed to keep good and evil in balance.

These stories portray Rangda as your classic outcast single woman, feared and reviled, partial to a dabble in demonic insanity and obsessed with her daughter's relationship status. But we can also see her as a woman who is locked in an eternal struggle to resist patriarchal demands and as a source of awesome power: ultimately, she is revered by villages for guarding them against demons. Balinese mythology is complex and nuanced; in these epic dances the flow of good and bad is reflected. The ritual restores harmony, but it offers only temporary resolution, just as life is complex and ever-changing.

So let's change the story. Shift the notion that being single means you are on a quest for true love, and explore a great relationship with yourself instead. Enjoying life on your own doesn't necessarily mean you're giving up on the idea of ever having a partner (if you want one), it's just that you're saying no to being defined by this. You don't have to be half of something to be whole. And if you've decided to uncouple, think about all the good stuff coming your way as a result of being single: throw yourself right into that amazing hobby – Calligraphy! Karate! Curling! – you'd abandoned in the blur of domesticity. Give more time to your friends and your family. Save up and travel wherever you want to, whenever (Bali looks nice), if you can. Single people shouldn't be treated like weird witches from the woods – and it's worth remembering that self-partnered Rangda wasn't in fact alone – as Calon Arang, she clearly had a close relationship with her daughter, and let's not forget about that army of *leyak* pals. Embrace solitude. Take yourself on a date. Get your fanciest pants on, book a killer restaurant and you do you. Never settle just for the sake of it, and make a great life of your own, on your own.

Beaivi

and Taking Care of Your Mental Health

SAMI, SCANDINAVIA AND RUSSIA

ALSO KNOWN AS

Beiwe, Beivve, Biejje

SKILLS

Bringing Light, Melting Butter,
Riding a Reindeer Zorb

RESPONSIBILITIES

Creation, Spring, Fertility, Sanity

Mental health issues affect around 450 million people worldwide. One in four people will be affected by a mental health disorder at some point in their life: it's one of the biggest causes of ill health globally. And the real kicker is that sub-optimal mental health is also terrible for our physical health: it messes up our immune system, it can lead to

under- and over-eating, self-medication through drugs and alcohol and self-harm – one study has shown it's even worse for us than smoking. And what's really sad is that nearly two-thirds of people with mental health issues never seek treatment.

We need to start valuing our beautiful minds just as much as we value our bodies, and we need to acknowledge the psychological injuries we all might face during our lives – loneliness, rejection, failure – just as we do our physical ailments. We should put them right at the forefront of our conversations, and recognise collectively that it's really not all in our heads. The Sami,* an ancient Finno-Ugric people still thriving today in Norway, Finland, Sweden and Russia, were way ahead of their time when it came to caring for those who weren't coping.

Sami culture stretches back over three millennia and the hundred thousand Sami who live in Scandinavia and Russia today work hard to protect it. Over previous centuries Sami culture came close to being wiped out thanks to oppression and the confiscation of territory by the dominant European political bodies.

* The Sami used to be known in other languages as Lapplanders – though they always referred to themselves as Sami. 'Lapp' means patch or scrap of clothing – the inbuilt offensiveness of the term lies in the implication that because of poverty, the Sami's clothing was patched together.

However, in 1989 a Sami parliament was appointed, giving important rights back to the people. In Norway and Sweden, for example, only the Sami are allowed to practice reindeer husbandry. Reindeer herding has always been a central part of Sami life and Sami mythology, steeped in animism and shamanism, reflects how heavily rooted in nature their culture was and still is. Before the Christianisation of the eighteenth century, animal spirits were worshipped, particularly bears and reindeer. The veneration of ancestors was also important. Some of the many Sami gods had similarities to Norse deities. While it can be a difficult culture to interpret from the outside, stories and songs still reflect the Sami's deep connection to the natural world around them.

The land that the Sami inhabit is extreme and seasons play a crucial role in how they live. There is a long, dark winter with hardly any daylight, so it's no wonder that Beaivi, the Sami goddess of the sun, spring and sanity, was so important, and the rituals surrounding her return after the winter so vital. Beaivi brings back life: with sunshine and daylight, plants grow, prosperity is reawakened – everything gets less chilly and everyone feels a bit more chill. In some depictions Beaivi is accompanied by her daughter Beaivi Neid and they travel together across the sky enclosed in a cool sphere of reindeer antlers;* in some art Beaivi even has antlers herself. The importance of the sun to the Sami people is visible in the design of their flag – one of the most stylish we've ever seen – which has a brightly coloured circle as a central element.

Every winter solstice, the Sami sacrificed a white female reindeer, or some other white animal, to Beaivi to encourage her to come back. After the sacrifice, the meat was threaded onto sticks and bent into circles – a kind of kebab garland, if you will – with the circle representing the sun. At the end of the winter, the Sami smeared butter over their doorsteps, to give Beaivi the strength to return. When the butter melted in the sunshine it signalled that she was on her way. On the summer solstice leaf rings were made and buttery recipes feasted on to celebrate her high point.

Alongside these rituals, the Sami also sent Beaivi prayers to help people suffering from mental health issues. They knew that those long, dingy winter months could cause depression and dark despair, and that Beaivi could bring happiness and optimism, and pull people out of the darkness, both literal and symbolic.

* Santa was not the first to use a reindeer vehicle for transport across the sky! The Baltic sun goddess Saule rides in a horse-drawn celestial chariot, much like the famous Greek sun god Helios and the Norse sun goddess Sól, who has the added incentive of being pursued by a wolf on her daily drive.

Seasonal affective disorder was only defined as a condition in the 1980s, but the Sami have been aware of it for centuries. Relatively recently it still wasn't taken seriously, but now health professionals recognise that overproduction of the sleepy hormone melatonin and a lack of the happy hormone serotonin, both of which are affected by exposure to sunlight, can cause depression. It's cheering to think about an ancient community putting mental health high on the agenda and cutting through the isolation of depression by supporting those around them.

Just as the Sami regularly used community rituals to protect and care for mental health, we can start practising daily mental health hygiene and rituals. Once you feel you are suffering, it can be very difficult to get yourself out of a spiralling thought process; it can feel like you are trapped in an endless winter. So how can you break the cycle of negative rumination – the act of chewing over thoughts endlessly – and convince yourself that Beaivi and her healing rays will at some point start to appear on the horizon? Don't tell yourself that your problems are not important enough – everyone needs and deserves a helping hand at times. Talk to your friends. Take sleep seriously: go to bed at a regular time each night. Try to manage stress, maybe give yourself ten minutes a day for deep breathing, meditation, reading, yoga or just staring out the window – whatever zens you out. Pay attention to your hormonal cycle. Take time to reflect. Keep active. Eat well. Don't drink too much, and, if you do, prepare yourself in case things seem negative and out of proportion the morning after. Recent evidence shows that going to the seaside (or any body of water, even a fountain) has a positive effect on our mental well-being. Perhaps follow the Japanese custom of forest-bathing by going for a walk under some trees. If you're not a nature kind of person, visit a gallery or museum (real or virtual) and be inspired. Accept the incredibly liberating concept that some things are simply outside of your control. Remember, no matter how bad things can seem, the world keeps turning, rolling through the seasons, and although winter is always coming, the sun also always rises.

Pele

and Keeping Your Cool

HAWAIIAN, HAWAII

ALSO KNOWN AS

She Who Shapes the Sacred Land, Madam Pele, Tutu Pele, Eater of the Earth, The Redness of Fire

SKILLS

Arguing, Throwing Rocks and Lava, Destroying Land, Creating Land

RESPONSIBILITIES

Fire, Lightning, Wind, Volcanoes

When was the last time you were completely furious? The last time you saw red or blew your top? Felt your eyes flashing and your blood boiling? The idioms we use to describe anger often call to mind the hot-tempered Hawaiian goddess of fire, Pele. When Pele lost her cool it wasn't just a metaphorical scorching burn that she'd let loose but a literal explosion of flames and molten rock.

According to the legends about her, Pele was always a firestarter. Born into the family of the top Polynesian gods descended from the earth goddess Papa and the sky god Wakea, she had to leave her home in the gods' land of Kahiki because she kept annoying her sister, the sea goddess Namakaokaha'i, by setting fire to things (in some versions she also sleeps with Namakaokaha'i's husband – Pele was 'hot' in every way). Pele was given a canoe by her oldest brother Kamohoali'i, the shark god, and set out with a gang of her other siblings to find a new home. This proved tricky as tenacious Namakaokaha'i kept inundating the islands she chose, until she found the Big Island of Hawaii, where Mauna Loa mountain was high enough to resist the sea goddess's efforts. Pele settled down here inside the cosy Halema'uma'u crater of the Kīlauea volcano, equipped with the ultimate in luxurious underfloor heating.

On the way from Kohiki to her new home in her canoe, Pele carried the unusual cargo of an egg, which she kept warm in her armpit. From this egg her favourite sister, Hiʻiaka the cloud goddess, hatched. Pele and Hiʻiaka were best buds until Pele's impatient temper got the better of her. Their conflict is one of the best-known stories about our favourite fiery goddess.

One night while sleeping, Pele heard the seductive sounds of the sacred hula dance coming from the nearby island of Kauai. Her spirit left her body and followed the music, where she found the chief Lohiau dancing. His moves impressed and she fell for him hard. They spent several passionate nights together before Pele's spirit had to rejoin her body.

When Pele returned to Kīlauea she asked Hiʻiaka to do her the favour of going to fetch Lohiau and bring him to her. She equipped her little sis with various helpful items (including a lightning skirt that sounds particularly cool) and said, 'Nothing shall block your road. Yours is the power of woman, the power of man is nothing to that.'* It was lucky that she set up Hiʻiaka so nicely because it turns out the journey to retrieve

* This account of Pele and Hiʻiaka was published in 1915 by a white doctor, and son of missionaries, Nathaniel B. Emerson, from stories told to him by Hawaiians. Emerson dedicated his book to Queen Liliʻuokalani, who was the last monarch of Hawaii before US annexation in 1898.

Lohiau was beset with trouble and danger and severely tested Hi'iaka's sisterly devotion, not least because Lohiau was dead when she arrived and she had to revive him. And then he turned out to be inconveniently attractive. But Hi'iaka had promised not to crack onto him, in return for Pele doing the goddess version of watering her plants while she was away – taking care of her sacred garden.

Unfortunately, Pele thought her sister's travels were taking suspiciously long and decided that Hi'iaka must be copping off with her beau. What's a fire goddess going to do when disrespected like this? When Hi'iaka returned home she found her garden burnt to the ground and her girlfriend, Hopoe, who liked to dance there, petrified in lava. Pretty cross herself now, Hi'iaka snogged Lohiau right under her sister's nose on the edge of the crater and Pele burned him to a crisp too.

In some versions this story has a happy ending, in which Pele revives Lohiau again (poor guy must not have known if he was coming or going) and allows him and Hi'iaka to go off together. Pele ends up in a volatile romance with the pig god of agriculture Kamapua'a instead. Their super-dysfunctional constant lava-throwing and trampling of the undergrowth together is considered responsible for Hawaii's uniquely beautiful, varied and fertile landscape.

Pele is an intense goddess who doesn't dig disrespect. Another story tells of how a chief called Kahawali was enjoying how great he was at sledging down a hillside, with everyone cheering him on, when an old lady appeared and challenged him to a race. He was dismissive of her and not long after found himself being pursued by a flaming angry goddess surfing down the slope behind him on her own river of burning lava. He had to leg it to a far-off island to escape her.

Given that Kīlauea is one of the most active volcanoes around, and was in a constant state of eruption between 1983 and 2018, frequently destroying homes and forests, it's no surprise that people still leave offerings for Pele at the edge of her crater (she's particularly keen on red ʻōhiʻa lehua flowers). A modern legend invented to protect the National Park has developed that says she's deeply offended by people who think they can nick off with a piece of her rock as a souvenir. The Hawaiian National Parks Service receives many packages of returned stones and lava each year with accounts from the pilferers of how much bad luck they have suffered since they nabbed them against Pele's will.* She still appears near her home, sometimes to

* Other noted underground goddesses with a strong line in vengeance (also the descendants of an earth goddess) are the Ancient Greek Erinyes, or Furies. They were so scary they were described as wearing

warn of impending trouble, often in the form of an old woman with a little white dog, smoking a cigarette.

Pele is a goddess who genuinely inspires awe – as anyone who's watched footage of volcanic eruptions would immediately realise. She is loved and feared in equal measure and is simultaneously a destructive and creative force – her eruptions have created seven acres of new land in the Hawaiian archipelago since 1983.* She is a symbol of the power of nature and the necessity of respecting it and not exploiting it too far.

There is something liberating in Pele's go-getting attitude and liberal venting of her emotions. Anger is an essential emotion that motivates us to change things that are unjust, but it is also an emotion that can be deeply destructive – as poor Hopoe found out – when not managed and expressed properly. And even the most justifiable and controlled expressions of anger can make people feel uncomfortable. Anger is perceived differently depending on who the angry person is,

dresses dripping with blood, having snake hair and bats' wings, and were referred to by the noa-name the Eumenides, or 'Kindly Ones', in order to avoid summoning them by accident – a bit like Voldemort.

* The New Zealand fire goddess Mahuika is often likened to Pele. She is the grandmother of the great Polynesian trickster god Maui, who has been brought to wide international fame by his appearance in the Disney film *Moana*, where he and the titular heroine compete with a raging volcano goddess who (spoiler alert) then turns into an abundant earth goddess, similar to Pele.

often being interpreted as more aggressive when expressed by people of colour and as a sign of mental instability when expressed by women. In many cultures, women have been encouraged to see 'niceness' as their ultimate goal, and expressions of emotions that ruffle the surface of the ideal feminine placidity have been interpreted as hysteria* and overreaction.

Given the way women are still widely diminished – by being paid less than their male counterparts, held to more demanding standards of physical appearance and parenting, subject to higher incidences of unwanted sexual innuendo and contact, and often asked to smile more while being expected to have unnaturally little body hair and wear clothes that don't have pockets – it would be weird if we weren't a bit angry. The trick is to strike a balance between an unhealthy suppression of rage and Pele's scorched-earth aggression. Find a safe space and allow yourself to really feel the things that bother you; it's OK to give in to that feeling of igneous ire rising inside you, to let the sparks of rage

* 'Hysteria' was widely considered to be a female condition, hence the word for it comes from the Greek word for 'uterus'. The jokey questions 'Time of the month?' and 'Got your period?' whenever a woman becomes cross have a similar basis and used to be very popular among men in the 1970s and 1980s. (Even though any hormone-induced irritability, PMT, occurs before a woman's period arrives and has usually passed by the time they are actually surfing the crimson wave.)

light the fire of change under you. Channel that righteous fury into creating a new, blossoming world for women and for us all. Burn bright!

Epona

and Learning to Be Adaptable

GALLO-ROMAN, CENTRAL EUROPE

ALSO KNOWN AS

Sancta Regina, Great Mare,
Divine Mare

SKILLS

Equine Care, Riding Side-Saddle
While Carrying a Fruit Platter

RESPONSIBILITIES

Horses, Fertility

Ah, Pony Girls. From *Black Beauty* to *My Little Pony*, many of us have felt a deep sympathy for our equine friends. Imagine how much more intense the bond between humans and horses was when we relied on them for our safety and food. In Gaul this was certainly the case. Gaul was an Iron Age territory which covered parts of what is now France, Belgium, the Netherlands, Germany and Italy, before it was finally conquered by the Romans under Julius Caesar in around 50 BCE (apart from Asterix's indomitable village, of course).

The Gauls' cavalry was famously most excellent and horses were also essential for their farming. Epona was the goddess they looked to for the protection of these precious animals. And horses were highly valued: they appeared on coins, there is evidence noble Gauls were buried with their steeds, and the famous Gaulish chieftain Vercingetorix is said to have sent his horses away to safety when under siege by the Romans so that they wouldn't fall into his enemies' hands. Many different cultures used to practise horse burial, and archaeological evidence of this has been found as far afield as Russia, Scandinavia and China. This may indicate both horses' practical value and the fact that they, and other animals, were sometimes considered psychopomps – a brilliant word meaning entities who guide the souls of the dead to the afterlife.

The cult of Epona was one of the most widespread from the Celtic-speaking world; hundreds of statues and inscriptions have been discovered by archaeologists. This is because she was enthusiastically adopted by the Romans who invaded Gaul and spread her worship through their vast empire. The Romans loved to mix, or syncretise, other religions with their own, like a fancy religious cocktail, but it was highly unusual for a Gaulish goddess to get the kind of pure adoption that she did – even landing her own feast day on 18 December.

All this came from mysterious beginnings. We don't have any substantial mythological accounts of Epona or her origins. The only story about her is an unedifying one recorded by an unknown third- or fourth-century Roman writer slagging off some random. It reads, 'Fulvius Stellus hated women and used to consort with a mare and in due time the mare gave birth to a beautiful girl and they named her Epona. She is the goddess that is concerned with the protection of horses.' Such romantic origins!

Epona is usually depicted calmly sitting on a horse, often deftly carrying bountiful fruit and other food, or with one or two foals gambolling alongside her.

She appears in carvings and small sculptures which were kept in stables and garlanded with roses, and is also mentioned in Roman inscriptions, including one on Hadrian's Wall. The depictions of her with foals and other animals are similar to those of the Greek forest-dwelling and hunting goddess Artemis (whom the Romans called Diana) in her role as Mistress of the Beasts, and the images where she is presented placidly riding side-saddle immediately call to mind the Christmas-card images of Mary, mother of Jesus, travelling to Nazareth on her donkey, the fruit basket in this instance being the special baby in her womb.

The few references to Epona in surviving Roman literature, such as in a poem by Juvenal, imply she was a goddess of the people, rather than a posh public deity. Juvenal refers to her in the context of describing a nobleman slumming it by worshipping her in his 'stinking stables' and another later poet, Prudentius, flags her humble status, writing, 'Nobody gives a throne above the stars to the goddess Cloacina [goddess of the sewers*], or Epona.'

* Weirdly, as well as being the goddess of sewer systems, Cloacina was the Roman goddess of marital sex and associated with Venus, the goddess of love. Go figure. Interestingly the Romans used to sometimes also keep shrines to the luck goddess Fortuna (see pp. 53–60) in their toilets. Both of these goddesses were more positive than Sulak, the Babylonian demon known as 'the lurker in the latrine', who brought on illness.

Epona's popularity spread because of her adoption by soldiers in the Roman cavalry and the postmen and stablehands who accompanied them. Many of these men were not native Romans but were employed from local areas. They were bonded by their jobs and their reliance and respect for their animals, on whom their lives depended. This makes it easy to see why Epona won her spurs with them, and also why she was carried across so much of the Romans' conquered territory. She is not a martial war goddess, like Athena, but rather a protector.

Horse worship was prevalent amongst nomadic, agricultural and martial communities, and links have been made between Epona and two other supernatural Celtic horse ladies. The first of these is the Irish Macha, one of the three sinister avatars of the Morrígan, who could run faster than horses. The second is the Welsh Rhiannon.

Rhiannon is a supernatural heroine in the *Mabinogion*, the great medieval Welsh collection of mythological stories. She appears to the hero Pwyll dressed in gold and sedately riding a white horse, but however hard Pwyll tries to catch up with her on his own steed, he can't. Rhiannon finally stops to talk to him when he speaks to her politely rather than chasing her down, as is completely understandable – although we would not advise stopping to chat to a man who has been tenaciously stalking you IRL. She then reveals that she's taken a shine to him even though she's supposed to be engaged to someone else, and they end up getting married. It's not all unbridled romance for the couple from this point on though. Rhiannon has a choice burn for Pwyll when he accidentally agrees to give her back to her previous fiancé* during a mix-up at a feast: 'Be silent as long as thou wilt. Never did man make worse use of his wits than thou hast done.'**

After this slight hitch, the couple lived in matrimonial bliss until Pwyll's mates started doing that annoying thing of saying, 'So, when are you guys going to have kids?' – except with more menace, as having an heir in those days was a crucial part of holding on to your authority. Bowing to peer pressure, Pwyll promised to divorce Rhiannon if she didn't get pregnant in the next year. Luckily, they had a little boy called Pryderi, who becomes a recurring character in other *Mabinogion* stories.

* Rhiannon's previous beau is intimidated into giving up his claim on Rhiannon after she contrives to have him bundled up in a bag and beaten with sticks by men who think he is a badger. This apparently explains the origins of the popular game 'Badger-in-the-Bag', which happily doesn't seem to be so popular any more.

** This is Lady Charlotte Guest's original translation from 1845. You'll find out more about Lady C. in the upcoming chapter on another Welsh heroine, Blodeuwedd (see pp. 195–203).

Unluckily, Pryderi went missing at birth while Rhiannon and all her maids were asleep. When the maids woke up, instead of telling the truth, they were so worried about getting in trouble that they killed a puppy and covered Rhiannon in its blood and told everyone that she had eaten her son. As you do. As punishment Rhiannon had to sit by the gates of the castle and carry any visitors up the drive on her back like a horse. Finally, a man called Teirnyon arrived accompanied by a child, refused her offer of a piggyback and explained that he had discovered an evil force stealing his foals and, when he attacked it, had found a baby boy, who he and his wife had been looking after. He'd brought the little fellow with him after hearing about Rhiannon's story. This is Pryderi, who is restored to his parents. Rhiannon's connection with horses and fertility is clear from this story, as is an interesting parallel between a horse's purpose – to roam the hillsides wild, free and lovely until it is bound in servitude and used as breeding stock – and a woman's at this time.

With Epona and Rhiannon we once again see that uneasy paradox where a female deity is identified with protection and generation as well as that fave goddess speciality: death. She who giveth can also taketh away. But what we want to focus on with these horse goddesses is the benefit of adaptability – not just in

Rhiannon's stalwart acceptance of her changing fate, but particularly in the way that Epona moved from being a goddess of a conquered people to a popular protective figure embraced by the conquerors and made more powerful and memorable because of this. This is also true of another great Irish goddess, Brigit, who preferred cows to horses and whose other specialities were fire, water and healing. Brigit was an ancient goddess but she was reinvented by the Catholic Church as one of the patron saints of Ireland, St Brigit.* Her pagan origins are given away by her feast day of 1 February, which was the date of the Celtic festival of Imbolc that marks the beginning of spring.

What is the secret to Epona's success? She made herself useful. Her area of expertise was central to the lives of many ordinary people at the time when her cult was prevalent. Epona remained relevant and open to interpretation but she had very clear and strong central values. She may not be well known today but

* Even further from her origins, Brigit has also been syncretised into Maman Brigitte or Gran Brijit, the sweary Vodou spirit of death. You can see her on telly in the adaptation of Neil Gaiman's novel *American Gods* along with many other great goddesses including Oshun, the Slavic star goddesses the Zorya, a character called Mama-ji, who is based on Kali, Easter, who is based on the German spring goddess Ostara, and Bastet, who appears both as a human and as a cat. Gaiman also invented some modern goddesses of his own, including Media, played by Gillian Anderson.

she is still referred to in odd places, such as Nintendo's *Legend of Zelda* video game, where the hero's horse is called Epona. Not bad going for a deity who we know was being worshipped nearly two thousand years ago. The world around us is changing at an ever-increasing pace and sometimes this can seem disorientating, but remember that you can always reinvent yourself for the times; just never lose the essence of who you are.

Green Tara
and Beating Fear

BUDDHIST, TIBET

ALSO KNOWN AS

The Embodiment of Wisdom,
Great Protectress, The Liberator,
Dolma (in Tibet), Khadiravani (Tara of the Forest), Syamatara, Sgrol-ma (in Tibet)

SKILLS

Delivering Hope, Saving People,
Wisdom

RESPONSIBILITIES

Optimism, Meditation,
Compassion

Parties. Public speaking. Flying. The dark. Buttons (yes, really)*. Phobias can trip us up – and fear can stop us from making big, potentially life-enhancing decisions, like quitting our jobs to set up our own businesses, or ditching that toxic frenemy who is always doing you down, or taking on a charity sky dive. A racing heart, tight throat, sweaty palms: no wonder it's called crippling, this anxiety business.

Tara – a goddess focused on actively helping people overcome their fears – is one of the most important and popular deities of Tibet, Mongolia and Nepal and is also revered by Buddhists in many other countries. Buddhism is notoriously hard to pin down: for some it is a philosophy, for some it's a culture. There are many different traditions, schools and practices carried out by its 520 million followers across the world. One commonality is its founder, Gautama Buddha, who lived in India around the sixth century BCE. His teachings are followed in most Buddhist traditions, based on the idea of breaking the human cycle of birth, suffering and death through achieving nirvana or by becoming a Buddha, or 'awakened one'.

Green Tara appears in many different schools of Buddhism – she's a female Buddha in Vajrayana

* Fear of buttons is called 'koumpounophobia'. You're welcome.

Buddhism, and is the female consort of the bodhisattva (Buddha-to-be) Avalokitesvara* in Mahayana Buddhism. These different branches of Buddhism emerged over centuries and developed in complex ways with individual monks' teachings, languages, beliefs and geographical areas. Green Tara was said to have been born from a single tear Avalokitesvara shed as he looked down from his heavenly perch at the suffering and horror of humanity below. A huge lake spread from that one tear, a lotus appeared and from inside it came the lovely Tara, bringing hope, optimism and bravery. Another story has her origin as a mortal princess who rejected monks' warnings that she needed to be reincarnated as a male figure in order to achieve full enlightenment. None of that for our Tara; she was determined to find enlightenment as a woman – just one great example of how she teaches us to overcome others' prejudices and negativity. The fourteenth Dalai Lama even name-checked her as a force for the feminist movement in Buddhism.

Tara has many forms. Tibetan temple banners often show as many as twenty-one Taras, in different colours

* The Dalai Lama is considered an incarnation of Avalokitesvara in Tibet. In China Avalokitesvara has been worshipped in male and intersex forms and is now usually venerated as the female goddess Guanyin (known as Kannon in Japan).

with different attributes. She's often depicted draped in jewels with an elaborate updo on a blue lotus, left leg thrust forward, ready to spring into action and help humanity. Green Tara is the most popular of all the Taras. She protects against bad energy – specifically, eight dangers, each of which is represented by an animal or immediate threat that corresponds to a negative or damaging human emotion. There is the lion of arrogance, the elephant of ignorance, the fire of hate, the snake of jealousy, the thief of wrong views, the bondage of avarice, the flood of lust, prisons and greed, and the demon of doubt – a vivid and proper roster of fear and loathing right there. So if it helps to consider your fear of being called on for your thoughts in meetings as a giant hyena, then follow Tara's path and feel free.

Tara is also a meditation deity, invoked as a focus in practice. Buddhists believe that calling on her can help liberate us from our worries and negativity. She can't make fears magically and literally disappear, but by teaching the *dharma* – the collective law that shows us the right way to live – and allowing us to understand the true nature of the universe, we can find respite from stress.

So here are our Tara-inspired strategies for coping when dread threatens to overwhelm you. First, try some meditation or mindfulness techniques – even if it is just taking some minutes to slow things down and concentrate on something other than the thing that is making you feel fearful; thinking about your breath moving in and out of your lungs can diminish panic. 'Flooding' is another technique: this involves maximum exposure to the thing you are afraid of. So, if you are seriously scared of buttons you'd find yourself a pearly queen and have a go at putting on their jacket. There are less extreme methods, too, like desensitisation. If you are terrified of public speaking maybe start by setting yourself the target of speaking up once in a meeting, or at your book club. You might then graduate to doing tiny, thirty-second talks with notes to your cat, then maybe without notes, and so on until you can stand up in front of a whole audience and feel OK about it. One useful tip is to remember that anything is bearable for ten seconds and work up from there.

Another powerful way to banish the jitters is to recognise, like wise Tara, that the anxiety is to do with your thoughts rather than reality. Tara shows us this in her use of a beast or mortal threat to represent a human emotion. Let's take the fear of flying as an example close to our hearts. First, hear and recognise when your perceptions are off: 'I must not fall asleep because if I do the plane will fall out of the sky' is scientifically untrue. Then look out for catastrophising, e.g., 'I may survive the plummeting bit but when the plane sinks into the sea I will definitely be eaten by a great white shark.' If you can repeat the mantra that this is a thought that you do not need, you are in control of your thoughts, and you can send those thoughts away, then you are halfway there.

One thing that Tara's existence acknowledges is that fear is everywhere. Everyone is scared of something – you are not alone. And feeling afraid is often a sign that you are expanding your horizons and stepping out of your comfort zone, which is the only way to live a full and evolving life. The key is facing fear and giving it the Green Tara light, not wishing it away.

Lilith
and Owning Your Sexuality

MESOPOTAMIAN AND JEWISH,
MIDDLE EAST

ALSO KNOWN AS

Lilu, Lilîth, The Lillin, Lamia

SKILLS

Infanticide, Seduction, Standing Up for Herself

RESPONSIBILITIES

Demon Production, Sexual Satisfaction

We're all good when it comes to female sexuality, right? Women's desires have never been more openly valued and discussed. Well, sort of. The orgasm gap is a real thing: straight women tend to reach climax LESS THAN 60 PER CENT OF THE TIME THEY HAVE SEX. For men, it's a much more reasonable 90 per cent. The imbalance is partly because the science of sexuality – like all science, literature, politics and art – has been dominated by men. Sixteenth-century anatomists thought the clitoris was an abnormal growth, and even until recently female ejaculation was considered a freaky-leaky myth. Women's bodies have long been considered uncharted territory, and the psychology of sex doesn't fare much better. For most of us, our first encounter with the idea of it comes at school, where the entire conversation is framed around how not to have a baby (culminating in a very graphic and bloody video of a woman giving birth to really put us off for ever).

In education, sexual activity that is not tied to reproduction is bound up with shame and guilt, especially for women. Vaginas and vulvas are not much discussed and society seems to want us to think they are untidy and dirty in their natural state – hence the popularity of Brazilian waxes and unnecessary 'intimate feminine' bodywashes. Vaginas are personified in several

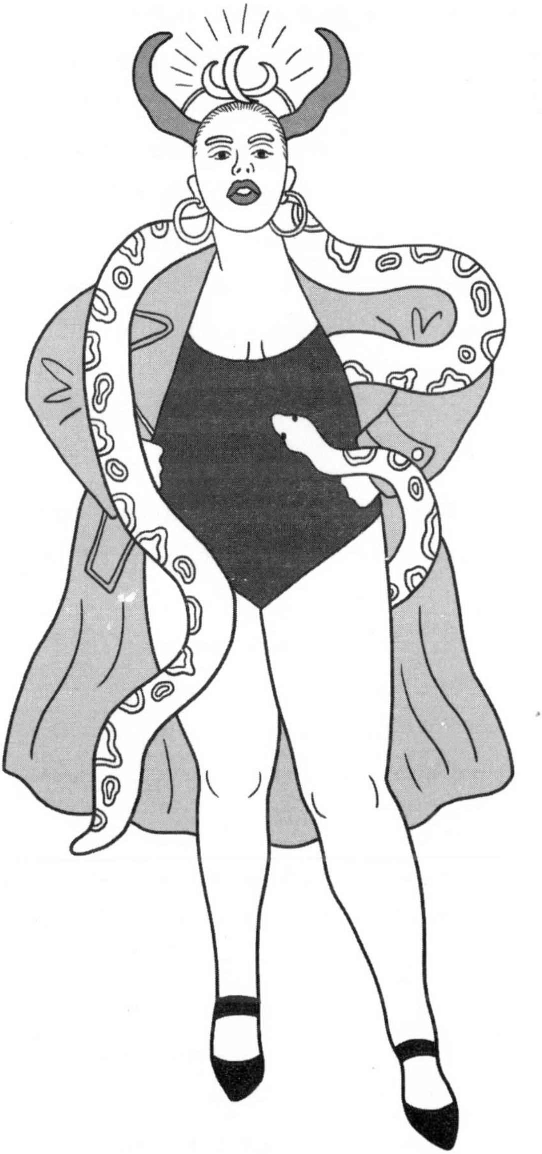

international myths, including tales from Asia, Africa and the Americas, as frightening, dark, man-eating entities which require taming by heroes: for example, in stories like that of the Jicarilla Apache vagina girls, who lived in a house decorated with vaginas* that ate men until a male hero came and gave them medicine to make their vaginas toothless.** Yet women should not be ashamed of their genitals, and sex and sexuality should feel like empowering forces for good.

One kick-ass character from ancient lore who quite literally refused to take things lying down is Lilith, a seductive demon who was considered in some traditions to have been Adam's first wife. Her history resists categorisation: for millennia she was cast as a terrifying spirit who strangled babies in their sleep and seduced snoozing men. Now, some scholars have reclaimed her as our very first feminist. She crops up in ancient Sumerian texts from the third millennium BCE

* Vulva-themed interior decor is a bold move but we can see it working: imagine a living room in delightful toning shades of Farrow and Ball Sulking Room Pink, Eating Room Red, Incarnadine, Deep Reddish Brown, Sand and Nancy's Blushes.

** This is what's known as a *vagina dentata* or 'toothed vagina' story. It might sound shocking but popular family film franchise *Jurassic Park* can be seen as a *vagina dentata* tale too – lots of female dinosaurs who are cleverer than you thought, have big dangerous teeth, a chaotic, reptilian attitude to life and no need for males in order to reproduce and dominate their environment: no wonder they need training by Chris Pratt.

– in the *Epic of Gilgamesh* she is scared out of a tree she's been lurking in which belongs to the great goddess Inanna. She appears in Ancient Egypt and Greece, and is mentioned once in the Bible in a grimly apocalyptic vision of the future in which it's imagined she'll be hanging out in the miserable end times. She's there in the Talmud as a succubus. Lilith is best known, though, through Jewish folklore and it's her gobsmacking performance in the medieval text *The Alphabet of Ben Sira* that cemented her reputation through the ages.

The Alphabet of Ben Sira is a satirical Hebrew text written around 700 CE. One theory is that Lilith's entry exists to solve a discrepancy in the creation myths in the Bible between Genesis 1 (where God creates men and women at the same time) and Genesis 2 (where woman is created as a helper for Adam in the Garden of Eden). In *The Alphabet of Ben Sira*, Adam had a first wife, Lilith, who like him was created from earth. They soon begin to argue – particularly over sex. One exchange ends with Lilith refusing to adopt the missionary position. She insists, 'I will not lie below,' and Adam replies, 'I will not lie below, but above, since you are fit for being below and I for being above.' Lilith does not comply. 'The two of us are equal, since we are both from the earth.' It's the ultimate battle of the sexes, in a terrible battle over sex. Eventually Lilith becomes so frustrated that she utters God's unutterable name, grows a pair of wings and flies away to the Red Sea in a rage, and is immediately recast as a demon capable of giving birth to hundreds of demon babies daily. Her act of transgression – insisting on her sexual equality – has extremely grave consequences. Adam then moves on with Eve and, as we know, that goes brilliantly too.* You begin to start wondering if the problem isn't with the wives.

Lilith as an archetype of the femme fatale, the sexy-yet-dangerous, demonised woman, has endured for centuries. Michelangelo depicted her as a coiled serpent in the Garden of Eden, Goethe had her in *Faust* as a dangerous temptress capable of ensnaring men with her hair, Rossetti focuses on her hair again in his famous painting *Lady Lilith*, where she is depicted in a state of self-admiration, and she crops up in James Joyce's *Ulysses* as the 'patron of abortions'. And in C. S. Lewis's *Chronicles of Narnia* the White Witch is said to be a descendant of Lady L. Lilith is also massive in popular culture. She's referenced in the 1980s and 1990s sitcoms *Cheers* and *Frasier*, where Frasier's icy ex-wife has her name. She also pops up in the current

* You can be reminded of Eve's scandalous snack – and the knowledge it brought her – every time you use an iPhone to google 'Is there really cyanide in apple seeds?' (There is.)

witchcraft series *Chilling Adventures of Sabrina*, where she refers to herself as Madame Satan, and in the horror show *Chambers*, where she inconveniently inhabits the central character's soul. A music festival was founded in her name in 1997, and she even features in *Scooby-Doo* and *The Fifth Element*, and has a song on Genesis's sixth album. Impressive work.

Different Liliths emerge for different writers. In Judith Plaskow's feminist retelling, *The Coming of Lilith*, she is created alongside Adam by God. Soon after she ups and offs. Adam complains to God, who makes him another woman, Eve, and for a time they live in harmony, until Eve and Lilith buddy up. The parable ends with Eve and Lilith as sisters in arms – full of ideas and possibilities – heading to Eden and an anxious and expectant Adam and Big G.

Lilith is a great weapon in the fight against patriarchal stereotypes. She is tenacious, powerful, and refuses to compromise sexually: she stands in direct opposition to the messages we heard as children in fairy stories, where happy endings come with a chaste kiss. She is complex and misunderstood, which makes her a potent feminist symbol, and perhaps explains why authors, filmmakers and songwriters have long been inspired by her. There are lots of ways to shake off whatever cloak of shame we might have around our sense of desire. One good starting point is to be a bit curious. Take a mirror and have a look at those hidden bits of your bodies. Talk about sex: studies show that women who talk to other women experience less anxiety when it comes to all things bedroom-related. Remember that Lilith shows that nobody should pressure you into anything sexual that you don't want. A healthy, joyful sex life is a wonderful thing: it's good for the heart, lowers blood pressure and relieves anxiety. However you do it, make sure that, in the spirit of Lilith, you do it on your own terms. That way, you'll always come out on top.

Blodeuwedd

and Finding Your Independence

WELSH, WALES

ALSO KNOWN AS

Flower Face

SKILLS

Persuasion, Adultery, Rebellion

RESPONSIBILITIES

Spring, Owls, Life and Death

Most of the literature that has captured the exploits of the goddesses in this book was created by men, and that is likely true of the earliest blossom of Welsh prose, the *Mabinogion*, which scholars believe was recorded by monks between the eleventh and twelfth century CE. (One appealing suggestion, which hasn't gained much traction in academic circles, is that it was actually written by the warrior princess Gwenllian, who died battling the Normans in Carmarthenshire in 1136.) The *Mabinogion* is a collection of a wide array of different oral legends from pre-Christian Wales, including some references to folklore A-lister King Arthur. The first full English translation was published alongside a Welsh transcription by the linguist, go-getter and driver of the Welsh Renaissance, Lady Charlotte Guest, in the nineteenth century.

The tale of Blodeuwedd is a story written down by a man about a woman created by a man. What makes the perfect woman? In the old days men found a pretty face and a nice passivity to be superhot and not much more was required. Blodeuwedd was made out of flowers – specifically 'the blossoms of the oak, and the blossoms of the broom, and the blossoms of the meadowsweet' – which produced 'a maiden, the fairest and most graceful that man ever saw'. (Being 'graceful' was a big qualification for women in the olden days, pretty much equivalent to having a double first in Engineering. That a trait that literally means they moved their limbs in a smooth and unruffled manner was so highly valued really hammers it home that women's role in society was to be quietly decorative.) Blodeuwedd's Dr Frankenstein was Gwydion, a

magician, who needed to create a non-human woman for his hero nephew Lleu to marry, due to an unfortunate curse the boy had received from his mother.

Blodeuwedd sprang into the world fully formed, fresh as a daisy, and immediately assumed the role of wife. And this was all she was supposed to be, a bit like a modern-day sexbot. It was very clear that she belonged to Gwydion and Lleu, her programmer and her owner. Today we angst about what might happen if the AI robots we build for our convenience one day turn against us (what horrors might await if Siri and Alexa go rogue?), and the story of Blodeuwedd casts an interesting light on these concerns. Her tale can be read as an expression of ancient anxiety about how dangerous and untrustworthy women can be if they aren't controlled – a common theme in many world myths, as we've read in the story of Lilith – and the destructive power of nature; although, to be fair, oak blossom and meadowsweet have rarely been involved in natural disasters. Blodeuwedd is also an example of the fear that someone who resists categorisation and exists on the borders between worlds can inspire.

Needless to say, Blodeuwedd's status as a perfect wife didn't last for ever. There is never a rose without a prick. One day, while her husband was away on business, our botanical beauty met a handsome guy called

Gronw Pebr and they fell instantly in love. The only way they could see to be together was to do away with Lleu, something Blodeuwedd doesn't seem to have expressed any qualms about – but, then again, who expects deep moral wrangling from a bouquet?

Unfortunately for Gronw and Blodeuwedd, murdering Lleu was a thorny issue. He was protected by magic, which meant that he could only be killed with a spear forged for a year on Sundays, while he was standing over a bath with one foot on a cauldron and one foot on a deer's back, under a thatched roof. He made sure it wasn't a situation he could accidentally find himself in after a few too many pints on a Friday night. Blodeuwedd used the classic cheating partner's excuse of being worried about him to wangle these conditions out of him, and when he filled her in on the details, she replied (we like to imagine with raised eyebrows), 'Well, I thank Heaven that it will be easy to avoid this.' However, she somehow persuaded him to enact this unusual pose, and Gronw stabbed Lleu in the midst of his cauldron–deer balancing act, causing him to turn into an eagle and fly away.

Gronw and Blodeuwedd took over Lleu's lands and moved in together, but they were not out of the woods yet. Gwydion made it his mission to hunt Lleu down, return him to human form, help him get his revenge and nip his wife's rebellion in the bud. When Lleu and Gwydion rocked up at the castle Blodeuwedd and her ladies-in-waiting scarpered, with all the ladies drowning in a lake in their haste to escape. (This lake is called Llyn Morwynion – Lake of the Maidens – and you can find it near Blaenau Ffestiniog in North Wales.) Gwydion eventually caught up with Blodeuwedd and told her ominously, 'I will not slay thee, but I will do unto thee worse than that.' He decided that transformation into an animal and public shame was the fate worse than death he was after. He turned Blodeuwedd into an owl, unable to show her face in the daylight and hated by all other birds. According to the story her name became the Welsh word for 'owl' from that point on.

In the past Blodeuwedd has been regarded as a cautionary tale about adultery and exceeding your brief, but modern readers respond positively to our floral rebel breaking free from male control. She is one of the most active female characters in the *Mabinogion* and, through her petal power, has become one of the best known. In the collection, her story follows tales of female shaming and humiliation that make it hard to resent Blodeuwedd's self-actualisation, and they also go some way to explaining the reason why her husband Lleu was cursed by his own mother.

The first of these tales of male exploitation begins with a young woman called Goewin, who has the unenviable job of looking after King Math of Gwynedd's feet. Math has been cursed to die if he isn't either out fighting or at home resting his battle-weary feet in a virgin's lap. One day when he's busy on the battlefield his nephews, tricky old Gwydion and his bad-seed brother Gilfaethwy, conspire so that Gilfaethwy can rape Goewin, which means that along with severe trauma she also loses her job. Math punishes Gwydion and Gilfaethwy creatively by making them shag each other as animals (deer, pigs and wolves) for three years, but then things go back to normal for them and they resume their roles at court. (Who knew that men in the public eye convicted of sexually exploitative behaviour towards women can eventually look forward to continuing their careers as before?) As it's an unmissable job opportunity, Gwydion encourages his sister Arianrhod to apply for the vacant foot-holding post.

Unfortunately, while Arianrhod's virginity is being publicly and magically tested by her brother, in front of her future boss, she gives birth to two boys, one of whom is Lleu. Arianrhod is so humiliated by her experience that when she finds out that Gwydion has adopted Lleu she curses her son so that he can never have a name, carry weapons or have a wife – the three things a real man desperately needed to succeed in Welsh society at this time. Gwydion finds a way around all of these conditions for Lleu, the last of which is Blodeuwedd, who he gets through on the technicality that she is actually foliage rather than a woman. So in the context of all this male bad behaviour it's hard to judge Blodeuwedd too harshly for simply coppicing off with a handsome stranger.

Blodeuwedd was not supposed to find her own independence but she surprised her owners by acting on her own desires, desires which they did not programme into her or intend for her to have the capability to realise. Looked at through one lens, she is the literal turf in a turf war between Lleu and Gronw. The fact that she moves through the states of being a vegetable, a person and then an animal makes her an obvious nature goddess and her magical birth and death symbolise the circle of life. Her association with flowers means she has also been identified as a spring or May Queen goddess.

All Blodeuwedd's flowery passive stuff, before her emancipation, also calls to mind the modern film trope of the manic pixie dream girl.* Blodeuwedd is literally

* The term 'manic pixie dream girl' was coined by the film critic Nathan Rabin in 2005. He described such characters as existing 'solely in the fevered imaginations of sensitive writer-directors to teach brood-

a 'pixie dream girl': her beauty and availability are key, and she has no past and no depth. And, most importantly, she exists in the plot purely to further her husband Lleu's story, first by cheering him up after his mother's curse as he can finally get a girlfriend, and then by providing his narrative low point before his great triumph over Gronw and his subsequent accession to the throne of Gwynedd.

However, the Blodeuwedd we choose to focus on is the herbaceous heroine who engineered her own blossoming, from a possession to a person, from a receptacle of desire to a participant, and from a side plot to one of the most compelling characters in folklore, who has inspired countless other works of art. So next time you feel like you are on the sidelines of your own story, rather than the central protagonist, make sure you take steps to follow your own ambitions, and then everything will come up roses.

ingly soulful young men to embrace life and its infinite mysteries and adventures'. After the term was used beyond its original intention, which was to point out sexist portrayals by male writers of one-dimensional female characters, Rabin retracted it in 2014.

Ix Chel
and the Importance of Old Ladies

MAYA, MEXICO AND CENTRAL AMERICA

ALSO KNOWN AS

Chac Chel, Lady Rainbow, Red Rainbow, Great End, Goddess O

SKILLS

Healing, Midwifery, Causing Floods, Fierce Fashion

RESPONSIBILITIES

Childbirth, Weaving, Divination, Medicine, Spiders

The old must make way for the new. The colonisers from Europe who landed in the Americas from the fifteenth century onwards certainly believed this. They were intent on 'civilising' the highly evolved civilisations they found there, and a central strut of this plan was replacing the continent's old gods and myths with Christianity. One of the highly sophisticated civilisations they messed with was the Maya.

The Maya population now numbers around seven million. Their ancestors were most prominent in Mesoamerica between 250 and 900 CE, inhabiting areas of what are now Mexico, Belize, El Salvador, Guatemala and Honduras. At their peak, the pre-Columbian Maya lived in large city-states of up to fifty thousand people with elaborate stone buildings, including their famously beautiful pyramid temples like those at Chichen Itza and Palenque in Mexico, which you can still visit today. They were a sophisticated, literate and religious people, whose knowledge of mathematics* and astronomy was vastly ahead of their time. Around 900 CE the great Maya cities declined and people moved back into agricultural villages (one of the cautionary reasons why academics think this happened was climate change,

* They grasped the concept of zero before anyone in Europe managed to get their head around it.

deforestation and overexploitation of natural resources by city dwellers). This is where they were living when Spanish explorers arrived on their shores in the sixteenth century, bringing disease and a conflict that lasted until 1697, when the invaders finally subjugated the indigenous population.

It was only in the twentieth century that Maya writing left on bark-paper manuscripts known as codices was properly interpreted, and this, along with carvings on their monuments and accounts left by Spanish scholars, is where we get our information about their gods. Only four legible codices survive today because the Catholic colonisers burnt everything they could find for idolatry. A particularly egregious culprit was Bishop Diego de Landa, who arrived in the Yucatán in 1549 and proudly incinerated shedloads of Maya books: 'We found a large number of books in these characters and, as they contained nothing in which there were not to be seen superstition and lies of the devil, we burned them all, which they [the Maya] regretted to an amazing degree, and which caused them much affliction.' Despite Diego's best efforts, veneration of the old gods remained and merged with the Catholic faith that spread throughout the Maya territories.

The pre-Columbian Maya worshipped over 165 gods and goddesses, mostly closely connected with the natural world and with overlapping characteristics or areas of expertise. Like other historic Mesoamerican religions, the Maya gods loved a bit of blood sacrifice and the Maya would go to war in order to capture victims to exsanguinate for their deities. They had a very complex calendar of rituals to observe and believed in cycles of world destruction and rebirth. One of the goddesses connected to these ideas of destruction and rebirth was Ix Chel.

Ix Chel is a hard goddess to pin down because scholars have spent some time arguing over surviving depictions of her and whether or not they all refer to the same goddess, or whether or not she was in fact a moon deity. However, she is most often known as the aged jaguar goddess of midwifery, which is a pretty cool handle. She appears in carvings as a clawed old woman, sometimes with a red body and jaguar eyes, a snake headdress, a skirt patterned with bones, and often carrying a water container. You would definitely notice her on the street.

There are many jaguar gods and goddesses in Mesoamerican myth because the jaguar was a very high-status animal: only the top brass could wear jaguar pelts. They were seen as creatures who could move between our world and the underworld because they hunted during the day and at night. Ix Chel was a top-tier goddess, and her cult centres on the islands of Cozumel and Isla Mujeres were noted by the Spanish invaders. Bad old Diego recorded that she was the goddess of childbirth and wrote that women going into labour would put icons of her under their beds. Her scary appearance also reflects the violence of childbirth,* and the fact that she is often depicted pouring water is seen by some as a reference to waters breaking during labour. Others see it as her ability to destroy the earth by flood if irked. The 'Chel' in Ix Chel's name has been interpreted to mean both 'rainbow' and 'end', linking her again to the underworld and destruction. Rainbows were not considered lovely, pretty treasure paths in Maya society but rather the product of demons: literally 'demon farts'.

In Maya culture, as in many others, midwives were a crucial part of society. This role was taken by experienced older women, who were also accorded more respect and religious privileges than their younger counterparts. Wisdom and experience are relevant to Ix Chel's other areas of patronage: weaving (she is sometimes depicted with top weaving animal the spider), medicine and divination. Ix Chel's scary old-ladyness means you'd probably avoid her on the bus, but also reflects how elderly women being separate from – and stepping outside their usefulness for – men therefore gain an intimidating independence. Without maternal responsibilities of her own Ix Chel

* The Maya's later northern neighbours, the Aztecs, gave special funeral honours to men who died in battle and women who died in childbirth, as the two were considered similarly heroic deaths. Their spirits were said to guide the sun on its path into the west each day, whereas everyone else went down into the underworld.

is free to put her prodigious energy into either helping (women in childbirth) or hurting (floods and storms).

Ix Chel is often described by mythology scholars as a 'crone' goddess. The word 'crone' and its close companion 'hag' most definitely have negative connotations. (See also some other lovely words for older women: 'bag', 'biddy', 'battleaxe', 'nag', 'witch'.) Crone in fact comes from the word 'carrion'. Charming.

In mythology and folklore crones are usually either helpful and grandmotherly or wicked and annoying (like Baba Yaga, pp. 71–7). In several Celtic stories men who treat hags with kindness and respect despite their obvious disgustingness are rewarded by the hag in question turning into a beautiful young woman. Cougar or jaguar, they often symbolise the closeness of death, so Ix Chel's midwife role makes sense in this context, as she is so crucial in the battle for life that takes place during labour.

As an elderly goddess of medicine and divination, Ix Chel also reminds us of a negative stereotype that has been very dangerous to women in the past. The medical expertise of experienced women was often valued, but the flipside of this, when such a woman transgressed social norms in some way, perhaps simply by not having a family around her, was the persecution of female healers as witches, which has taken place in cultures as far apart as Europe, Africa and India. Many see the persecution of so many women as witches as an indication of a patriarchal society's fear of independent women, particularly when they gather in groups. (Forget the Bechdel test, women gathered together are *bound* to be talking about men behind their backs and plotting some outrageous affront to male dignity, like bringing in laws to stop men taking pictures up their skirts!) Beyond exerting their power in a destructive way, women accused of witchcraft were also often accused of sexual transgressions, connecting to male fear of female sexuality. ('Shit, what if they're *not* actually all together plotting over their Pinot Grigio? What if they are really at various boutique hotels with their gigolos?') In later centuries, after mobs' fondness for the bonfire and the ducking stool waned, unusual women were often locked up in mental institutions if society couldn't get a handle on them.*

In more recent times, older women are less likely to be imprisoned or burned at the stake and more likely to be ignored or portrayed in stereotypical ways which point to their irrelevance and their lack

* Before legal reforms, women in the Victorian era who rebelled against their domestic destiny could be declared insane and committed to an asylum on the say-so of their husbands or fathers.

of attractiveness or glamour. Given it's accepted that they are no longer sufficiently decorative, the general idea is that if they're over fifty women should disappear – and if they draw too much attention to themselves they are likely to be met with embarrassment or suspicion. Happily this is changing and the post-menopausal life and beauty of women is being increasingly embraced and depicted in the same richness and complexity as fifty-plus men's has been for a long time. In many societies older women are revered, along with older men, as founts of wisdom, and enjoy greater social freedoms, independence and confidence than younger people.

Set free from the constraints of their fertility function, older women can be just as sexual, attractive, interesting and complex as anyone else. Despite her love of weaving, Ix Chel is by no means a boring goddess who sits back in the shadows with her knitting. She is a wise, vibrant contributor to the lives of younger people and her community. In her confident old age she sees life and death up close and can impart a valuable sense of perspective to all the less critical things that obsess us day to day. So next time you see your granny, make sure you really talk to her as a person, ask for her advice, find out about her experience, buy her a snake headband or a crossbones skirt. Seek out experienced mentors at work or in your community who you can learn from. Treat the older people around you with respect and attention. Forget silver foxes: old jaguar ladies rock.

Conclusion

> 'Am I not a goddess, and have I not protected you throughout in all your troubles?'
>
> Athena to Odysseus in Homer's *Odyssey*

We hope you've enjoyed reading our tour of some of the most outstanding goddesses of the world as much as we have enjoyed writing it. Our immortals have fired up our curiosity, snapped our synapses and illuminated our days with their divine glow as we've travelled to distant corners of the globe and seen how, over and over, myths and stories raise timely and enduring questions about women's roles, about our hopes and dreams and about the assumptions society makes about us. And while many of the stereotypes we still live with today have ancient origins, our deities can point us in new directions and tell us something new and vital about our own times.

In the same way that humanity has always used myth and religion to make sense of a baffling and brutal world, we can use the stories of the goddesses to guide us and liberate us from the constraints of mortal expectations today. As the writer and academic

Patricia Monaghan said, 'The goddess has never been lost. It is just that some of us have forgotten how to find her.' Many of the goddesses here still sustain and guide adherents to the religions they belong to, but even the more distant deities can help us. It may seem like there's nothing to be learnt from thousands-of-years-old obsolete objects of worship, but all our goddesses are damned tenacious. Through history they have evolved and changed to fit the times – from Athena and Aphrodite becoming more sedate in their Roman incarnations, to Pachamama and Pele being embraced by environmental campaigners today.

In revisiting these most ancient of ladies, we've attempted to remember their primeval powers. We've been thrilled to see goddesses trampling over boundaries and demanding respect in unexpectedly visceral, direct and, dare we say it, modern ways – witness Freyja's dogged pursuit of her necklace while smashing sexual convention, or the Selkie Wife's rejection of domestic drudgery in favour of the wild waves. Or how Baba Yaga rides her pestle and mortar as an inventive mode of transport, how Inanna goes after what she wants, or Blodeuwedd undermines the idealised blow-up-doll construct of a sexy woman and simply can't be controlled. None of the deities in these pages turned out to be the floaty, ethereal daisies we initially had in mind (and as they have been depicted over time). Our immortals are fierce and fantastic, they deploy their cunning and wit to get just what they want, and they unleash ferocious, spectacular, earth-quaking power. For that, we salute them.

One of the joys for us in writing this book has been tracking the unexpected connections between goddesses who were worshipped in countries thousands of miles and countless centuries apart. There are themes in their stories that arise again and again. Who knew snakes were such a thing? That flashing your undercarriage was considered a sure way to make another girl laugh in both Ancient Greece and Japan? That everyone used to think about incest so much? We've come across a lot of trees, birds, eggs, blood, transformations, journeys, secret knowledge, dying gods, hairdos, dancing, jewellery, floods and cats. But particularly snakes. So many snakes.

Pachamama, Tiamat and Baba Yaga's serpent forms, the Wawilak Sisters' devourer, Ix Chel's snakey headdress and Athena's shield are just the tip of the python when it comes to herpetological heroines. Others include biblical Eve in the garden of Eden with her flexible friend; the Greek goddess of health Hygeia and her medicinal serpent companion; Nüwa the Chinese snake-bottomed goddess; Benten the Japanese dragon goddess of good luck; Coatlicue the Aztec snake goddess; the great Python who in Greek mythology guarded the shrine of the earth goddess, Gaia; the Irish Caoránach, who was defeated by St Patrick; and, of course, the visual vocabulary of Taylor Swift. Snakes have long been associated with fertility, rebirth and danger. As have women. Scholars have come up with various theories to explain their popularity: they curl into circles (as in the famous Ancient Egyptian ouroboros symbol) and slough their skin, reflecting the eternal cycle of life and death; they are phallic-shaped and disappear into burrows in the earth, mimicking the act of heterosexual reproduction and so signifying fertility. And the ubiquity of fertility in these stories is unmissable; it's another theme that comes up again and again.

A huge number of goddesses are in some way linked to fertility or motherhood. Of course this makes sense in terms of pregnancy being a womb-based occupation, so they are a natural choice when you're looking round the room picking everyone's area of expertise: 'Apollo, yes, I'm making you manager for Music, Medicine, all that educated middle-class stuff; Poseidon, great to have you on board for the Ocean and Earthquakes, would you mind taking Horses too? Cheers. Hermes is on Comms, Hades on Death . . .

and Hera, Demeter, Aphrodite, Gaia and Persephone, why don't you ladies take Fertility? And, yes, you too, actually, Artemis. I know you're a confirmed singleton, celibate and just want to go for long walks in the woods with your dogs, but let's give you Childbirth anyway.' Pretty much only Athena escapes.

Don't get us wrong, fertility is a wonderful department to be in charge of: all those lovely plants and animals, the survival of our species and the whole cycle of life on the planet depend upon it. We're not against food and grandkids at all. But it can get a little samey for our divine ladies to always be associated so strongly with the anatomical fact that they have wombs. Luckily, they manage to combine such a vast array of other specialisms with the big F that it never gets dull. In particular, on the cycle-of-life front, they are often the deities who help humans wrestle with ideas of death. And this shows something else about many of our goddesses: they encompass oppositions, they reject binary distinctions, they mix up archetypes. Free from the bonds of mortal rules, goddesses can shapeshift from male to female, they can love women, men or both, they can be promiscuous or asexual, they can bring both comfort and tribulation, both life and death. And in doing so they bring a sense of wholeness. In their sparkly divine way, they reflect the complexity and contrasts, the highs and lows of our very human existences. They might not always die themselves but in their struggles and triumphs they show us that we can only truly appreciate the light if we witness the darkness.

The darkness of life in the times when these goddesses first came to prominence was quite different to what we face today. Despite recent events, we are generally far less likely than our ancestors to fall victim to the uncontrollably destructive natural disasters embodied in goddesses like Pele. Sugar, car accidents and suicide pose a greater threat to the majority of humans in the twenty-first century than war and lack of food. However, the world is still an unstable place for humans, and we can understand why these goddesses offered comfort and hope to their devotees in times when floods, famine, war and disease were far more common and widespread than they are today. Yet alongside the ways that goddesses can enlighten us about matters of life and death, it is also amazing how clearly they speak to us across millennia about relationships, family and fulfilment.

Despite our obvious chasms in experience, there's something hugely comforting in knowing that across the ages as far back as 4000 BCE the same elements have connected humanity's hopes and fears. Beaivi reflects our struggles with mental health; Inanna our wish to succeed; Bastet our urge to support each other; Kali our struggle with self-control; Aphrodite our need for love and connection. In a time of polarisation and division it is calming to see in world mythology that there is so much that binds humanity together.

But if there's one thing that struck us most about the cultures that worshipped, and still worship, goddesses, it is that so many of them seem so ahead of the current times in the way that they approach our environment. The old fertility speciality means that many of the goddesses in this book are directly associated with nature – whether in the form of the Earth itself like Pachamama, forest-dwellers like Baba Yaga or animals like Epona – and ancient worship of them necessarily involved reciprocity, respect and reverence. Their stories involve less of a sense of 'man's' dominance over nature. We may think we've 'progressed' and 'evolved' so far from the historical cultures our goddesses originally inhabited, but it's interesting to see how the pendulum has swung back in their direction recently.

These divine females have taught us not just about how to do better as women in a patriarchal world but also how to be better humans. The other theme that runs through this book is that of transformation. Our goddesses show that change isn't just possible, it's inevitable. And all of us have the power to make things better: we can all move the dial in the right direction and we don't need supernatural abilities to do it.

Pronunciation Guide

Here is a rough guide to some of the most common ways to pronounce the names in this book.

Amaterasu Ah-meh-ter-asu

Aphrodite Afro-*die*-tee

Arachne Ar-*ak*-nee

Ares *Air*-eez

Artemis *Ar*-te-miss

Athena Ath-*ee*-na

Badbh Bive

Beaivi *Bye*-vee

Blodeuwedd Blo-*die*-weth

Cú Chulainn Ku-hu-*layn*

Demeter Dem-*eet*-er

Dionysus Die-on-*ee*-sos

Dumuzi Du-*moo*-zee

Epona E-*poh*-na

Ereshkigal *Eresh*-ki-gahl

Freyja *Fray*-ya

Gilfaethwy Gil-*feeth*-wee

Gronw Pebr *Gron*-u Pebr

Gwydion *Gwid*-yon

Gwynedd *Gwyn*-eth

Hephaestus Hef-*eye*-stuss

Hera *Here*-uh

Hi'iaka Hee-ee-ah-ka

Inanna In-*nah*-nah

Ix Chel Eesh-*chel*

Kali Kah-*lee*

Kamapua'a Kah-mah-poo-ah-ah

Lakshmi *Lahk*-shmee

Macha *Ma*-cha

Mazu Mah-zoo

Medb Mayv

Morrígan *Mor*-ee-gan

Nemain *Ne*-vin

Olodumare Ollo-doo-*mahr*-ay

Orisha Oh-*ree*-sha

Oshun Oh-shoon

Pachamama *Pah*-cha-mama

Pele *Pear*-lay

Poseidon Poss-*eye*-don

Pryderi Pri-*dare*-ee

Pwyll Pwilth

Sekhmet Sekk-met

Tlaltecuhtli Tlal-tay-*coot*-lee

Tyche *Tie*-key

Uzume Uh-zoo-may

Yurlunggur *Yur*-lun-ger

Zeus Zyoos

Sources

GENERAL

Encyclopedia of Goddesses and Heroines by Patricia Monaghan, New World Library, 2010, 2014.

The Oxford Companion to World Mythology by David Leeming, Oxford University Press, 2009.

Goddesses and Monsters: Women, Myth, Power, and Popular Culture by Jane Caputi, University of Wisconsin Press, 2004.

The Faces of the Goddess by Lotte Motz, Oxford University Press, 1997.

Dancing with Goddesses: Archetypes, Poetry and Empowerment by Annis Pratt, Indiana University Press, 1994.

Conversing on Gender by G. G. Bolich, Psyche's Press, 2007.

Goddesses Who Rule, edited by Elisabeth Benard and Beverly Moon, Oxford University Press, 2000.

Goddess in the Grass: Serpentine Mythology and the Great Goddess by Linda Foubister, Spirrea Publishing, 2011.

Animal by Sara Pascoe, Faber, 2019.

The Woman's Companion to Mythology by Carolyne Larrington, Pandora, 1992.

Rage Becomes Her: The Power of Women's Anger by Soraya Chemaly, Atria, 2019.

Goddesses: Mysteries of the Feminine Divine by Joseph Campbell, New World Library, 2013.

Women and Power: A Manifesto by Mary Beard, Profile, 2017.

Legendary Ladies: Fifty Goddesses to Empower and Inspire You by Ann Shen, Chronicle, 2018.

A Short History of Myth by Karen Armstrong, Canongate, 2018.

The Concept of the Goddess by Sandra Billington and Miranda Green, Routledge, 1996.

Goddesses in Everywoman: Powerful Archetypes in Women's Lives by Jean Shinoda Bolen, HarperCollins, 2014.

'Soul Sex: Queer and Androgynous Deities' by Drake Bear Stephen, in *SoulSex: The Alchemy of Gender and Sexuality*, Wisdom Weaver Press, 2015.

Cassell's Encyclopedia of Queer Myth, Symbol, and Spirit: Gay, Lesbian, Bisexual, and Transgender Lore by Randy P. Conner, David Hatfield Sparks and Mariya Sparks, Cassell, 1997.

Myths of Greece and Rome by Thomas Bulfinch, Viking, 1979.

World Mythology: The Illustrated Guide, edited by Roy Willis, Duncan Baird, 1993.

Goddesses in World Culture, Vol. 1: Asia and Africa, edited by Patricia Monaghan, Praeger, 2010.

'Patriarchy and the Power of Myth: Exploring the Significance of a Matriarchal Prehistory', undergraduate senior project by Grace Varada Brandmaier, Bard College, 2015.

The Silence of the Girls by Pat Barker, Hamish Hamilton, 2018.

Circe by Madeline Miller, Bloomsbury, 2019.

Evolution of Goddess: A Modern Girl's Guide to Activating Your Feminine Superpowers by Emma Mildon, Atria, 2018.

APHRODITE

Aphrodite and Venus in Myth and Mimesis by Nora Clark, Cambridge Scholars Publishing, 2015.

Aphrodite, Gods and Heroes of the Ancient World by Monica S. Cyrino, Routledge, 2010.

Brill's Companion to Aphrodite edited by Amy Claire Smith and Sadie Pickup, Brill, 2010.

Goddesses, Whores, Wives and Slaves: Women in Classical Antiquity by Sarah B. Pomeroy, Bodley Head, 1975, 2015.

The Sacred Marriage of a Hindu Goddess by William P. Harman, Indiana University Press, 1989.

ATHENA

'I Hate Strong Female Characters' by Sophia McDougall, *New Statesman*, 15 August 2013.

Theoi Project, www.theoi.com

BABA YAGA

Baba Yaga, The Wild Witch of the East in Russian Fairy Tales, edited by Sibelan Forrester, Helana Goscilo and Martin Skoro, University Press of Mississippi, 2013.

Women Who Run with the Wolves: Contacting the Power of the Wild Woman by Clarissa Pinkola Estés, Rider, 1992.

BASTET

'Sekhmet: Patron Goddess of Healers and Physicians' by Sofia Aziz, *Nile Magazine*, December 2017–January 2018.

The Routledge Dictionary of Egyptian Gods and Goddesses by George Hart, Routledge, 2005.

'Why Ancient Egyptians Loved Cats So Much' by James MacDonald, *JSTOR Daily*, 27 November 2018.

BEAIVI

'The Decline of the Sámi People's Indigenous Religion' by Alan 'Ivvár' Holloway, University of Texas at Austin.

By the Fire: Sami Folktales and Legends by Emilie Demant Hatt, University of Minnesota Press, 2019

BLODEUWEDD

The Mabinogion, translated by Lady Charlotte Guest, Tonn Press and Longmans, 1849.

EPONA

'Epona: A Celt Among the Romans' by Katheryn M. Linduff, *Latomus*, vol. 38, 1979.

The Celts by Alice Roberts, Heron, 2015.

www.epona.net

FORTUNA

The Tradition of the Goddess Fortuna in Roman Literature and in the Transitional Period by

Howard Rollin Patch, College Studies in Modern Languages, 1922.

'The Cognomina of the Goddess "Fortuna"' by Jesse Benedict Carter, *Transactions and Proceedings of the American Philological Association*, vol. 31, 1900.

Fortuna: Deity and Concept in Archaic and Republican Italy by Daniele Miano, Oxford University Press, 2018.

FREYJA

Freyja, Lady, Vanadis: An Introduction to the Goddess by Patricia M. Lafayllve, Outskirts Press, 2006.

Norse Mythology by Neil Gaiman, Bloomsbury, 2018.

GREEN TARA

A Short Practice of Green Tara by Lama Zopa Rinpoche, FMPT, 2000.

Buddhism Plain and Simple by Steve Hagen, Penguin, 1992.

INANNA

Inanna: Queen of Heaven and Earth by Diane Wolkstein and Samuel Noah Kramer, HarperCollins, 1983.

Myths from Mesopotamia: Creation, The Flood, Gilgamesh and Others by Stephanie Dalley, Oxford World Classics, 2008.

IX CHEL

'The Birth Vase: Natal Imagery in Ancient Maya Myth and Ritual' by Karl Taube, in *The Maya Vase Book*, edited by Justin Kerr, Kerr Associates, 1994.

History in Infographics: The Mayans by Jon Richards and Jonathan Vipond, Wayland, 2016.

Ancient Maya Women by Traci Ardren, Altamira, 2002.

'The Major Gods of Ancient Yucatan' by Karl Taube, *Studies in Pre-Columbian Art and Archaeology*, no. 32, 1992.

'Ix Chel: Mayan Goddess(es) of the Moon, Fertility and Death' by K. Kris Hirst, *ThoughtCo*, 22 February 2019.

Star Gods of the Maya: Astronomy in Art, Folklore, and Calendars by Susan Milbrath, University of Texas Press, 1999.

The Cosmos of the Yucatec Maya: Cycles and Steps from the Madrid Codex by Merideth Paxton, UNM Press, 2001.

KALI

Encountering Kali: In the Margins, at the Center, in the West, edited by Rachel Fell McDermott and Jeffrey J. Kripal, Motilal Banarsidass, 2005.

Kali: The Feminine Force by Ajit Mookerjee, Thames and Hudson, 1988

LILITH

Lilith – The First Eve: Historical and Psychological Aspects of the Dark Feminine by Siegmud Hurwitz, Daimon Verlag, 2008.

The Coming of Lilith: Essays on Feminism, Judaism and Sexual Ethics, 1973–2003 by Judith Plaskow, Beacon Press, 2005.

MAZU

'Growth of the Mazu Complex in Cross-Straits Contexts' by Pamela J. Stewart and Andrew Strathern, *Journal of Ritual Studies*, vol. 23, no. 1, 2009.

The Mazu Beliefs and Customs, Unesco documentary, 2008, http://www.unesco.org/archives/multimedia/document-334.

MORRÍGAN

The Cattle-Raid of Cualnge (*Táin Bó Cuailnge*), translated by L. Winifred Faraday, David Nutt, 1904.

'Noínden Ulad: The Story of Macha', translated by Isolde Carmody, edited by Vernam Hull, *Celtica*, vol. 8, 1968.

The Celtic Myths: A Guide to the Ancient Gods and Legends by Miranda Aldhouse-Green, Thames and Hudson, 2015.

'War Goddess: The Morrígan and Her Germano-Celtic Counterparts', PhD thesis by Angelique Gulermovich Epstein, University of California, 1998.

OSHUN

African Religions: A Very Short Introduction by Jacob K. Olupona, Oxford University Press, 2014.

Osun Across the Waters: A Yoruba Goddess in Africa and the Americas by Joseph M. Murphy and Mei-Mei Sanford, Indiana University Press, 2001.

'The Philosophy of the Yoruba' by Yemi D. Ogunyemi, *Britannica Online*, 2015.

Yoruba Culture: A Philosophical Account by Kola Abimbola, Iroko Academic Publishers, 2005.

Religion, Food, and Eating in North America, edited by Benjamin E. Zeller, Marie W. Dallam, Reid L. Neilson and Nora L. Rubel, Columbia University Press, 2014.

Queering Creole Spiritual Traditions: Lesbian, Gay, Bisexual, and Transgender Participation in African-Inspired Traditions in the Americas by Randy P. Conner with David Hatfield Sparks, Harrington Park Press, 2004.

PACHAMAMA

'Virgin Mary/Pachamama Syncretism: The Divine Feminine in Early-Colonial Copacabana' by Lynette Yetter, *Western Tributaries*, vol. 4, 2017.

'Peru, Pachamama and Anthropological Functionalism', unpublished paper by J. Chavez-Cuellar, Biola University, 2018.

'Between Pachamama and Mother Earth: Gender, Political Ontology and the Rights of Nature in Contemporary Bolivia' by Miriam Tola, *Feminist Review*, vol. 118, 2018.

'Whither the Womb? Myths, Machines, and Mothers' by Amadeo F. D'Adamo, Jr, and Elaine Hoffman Baruch, *Frontiers: A Journal of Women Studies*, vol. 9, no. 1, 1986.

PELE

From Girl to Goddess: The Heroine's Journey through Myth and Legend by Valerie Estelle Frankel, McFarland and Co., 2010.

Pele and Hiiaka: A Myth from Hawaii by Nathaniel B. Emerson, Charles E. Tuttle, 1978.

RANGDA

Balinese Dance, Drama and Music: A Guide to the Performing Arts of Bali by I. Wayan Dibia, Runcina Ballinger et al., Periplus Editions, 2005.

Rangda: Bali's Queen of the Witches by Claire Fossey, White Lotus, 2008.

SEDNA

'The Inuit Sea Goddess', Masters thesis by Nelda Swinton, Concordia University, 1985.

The Central Eskimo by Franz Boas, Sixth Annual Report of the Smithsonian Bureau of Ethnology, 1888.

'An Analysis of the Central Eskimo Sedna Myth' by John F. Fisher, *Temenos*, vol. 11, 1975.

The Inuit Imagination by Harold Seidelman and James Turner, Thames and Hudson, 1994.

'The Story of Nuliajuk', narrated by Peter Irniq, Canadian Museum of History, www.historymuseum.ca/history-hall/origins.

'Women and Their Hair: Seeking Power Through Resistance and Accommodation' by Rose Weitz, *Gender and Society*, vol. 15, 2001.

Arctic Journeys, Ancient Memories: Sculpture by Abraham Anghik Ruben by Bernadette Driscoll Engelstad and William W. Fitzhugh, Smithsonian Arctic Studies Center, 2012.

'Breath-Soul and Wind Owner: The Many and the One in Inuit Religion' by Daniel Merkur, *American Indian Quarterly*, vol. 7, 1983.

Belief and Worship in Native North America by Åke Hultkrantz, Syracuse University Press, 1981.

'The Feminist Sedna: Representing the Sea Woman in Contemporary Inuit Art' by Victoria Nolte, *Aboriginate*, March 2015.

'The Sedna Cycle: A Study in Myth Evolution' by H. Newell Wardle, *American Anthropologist*, n.s., vol. 2, 1900.

Northern Voices: Inuit Writing in English, edited by Penny Petrone, University of Toronto Press, 1988.

'The Goddess of the Sea: The Story of Sedna' by James Houston, in *Canadian Encyclopedia*, 2015.

'The Sedna Cycle: A Study in Myth Evolution' by H. Newell Wardle, *American Anthropologist*, n.s., vol. 2, no. 3, July–September 1900.

SELKIE WIFE

Orkney Folklore and Sea Legends by Walter Traill Dennison, Orkney Press, 1995.

TANIT

History of the Phoenician Civilisation by George Rawlinson, e-artnow, 2018.

'Two Tales of One City: Data, Inference and Carthaginian Infant Sacrifice' by J. H. Schwartz, F. D Houghton, L. Bondioli and R. Macchiarelli, Cambridge University Press, 2017.

UZUME

'Are Men Funnier than Women, or Do We Just Think They Are?' by J. Hooper, D. Sharpe and S. G. B. Roberts, *Translational Issues in Psychological Science*, vol. 2, no. 1, 2016.

'Gender and the Evaluation of Humor at Work' by J. B. Evans, J. E. Slaughter, A. P. J. Ellis and J. M. Rivin, *Journal of Applied Psychology*, vol. 104, no. 8, 2019.

'Making Jokes During a Presentation Helps Men but Hurts Women' by Jonathan Evans, Jerel Slaughter, Aleksander Ellis and Jessi Rivin, *Harvard Business Review*, 11 March 2019.

WAWILAK SISTERS

Journey into Dreamtime by Munya Andrews, Ultimate World Publishing, 2019.

'Menstruation and the Origins of Culture: A Reconsideration of Levi-Strauss's Work on Symbolism and Myth', PhD thesis by Chris Knight, University College London, 1987.

Aboriginal Mythology, An A–Z Spanning the History of Aboriginal Mythology from the Earliest Legends to the Present Day by Mudrooroo, HarperCollins, 1994.

Myths of Dreaming: Interpreting Aboriginal Legends by James Cowan, Prism, 1992.

'The Myth of the Wawilak Women', in *A Black*

Civilization: A Social Study of an Australian Tribe by W. Lloyd Warner, Harper, 1957.

'Australian Aboriginal Peoples' by Ronald M. Berndt and Robert Tonkinson, *Britannica Online*, 2008.

Understanding Country: The Importance of Land and Sea in Aboriginal and Torres Strait Islander Societies by Dermot Smyth, Council for Aboriginal Reconciliation, 1994.

'Aboriginal Histories, Aboriginal Myths: An Introduction' by Jeremy Beckett, *Oceania*, vol. 65, 1994.

The Little Red Yellow Black Book: An Introduction to Indigenous Australia by Bruce Pascoe, Australian Institute of Aboriginal and Torres Strait Islander Studies, 2012.

'Dust Echoes: The Wagalak Sisters', study guide by Robert Lewis, Australian Teachers of Media, 2007.

'Levi-Strauss and the Dragon: *Mythologiques* Reconsidered in the Light of an Australian Aboriginal Myth' by Chris Knight, *Man*, n.s., vol. 18, no. 1, 1983.

'Myth as Language in Aboriginal Arnhem Land' by

R. Layton, *Man*, n.s., vol. 5, no. 3, 1970.

A Place for Strangers: Towards a History of Australian Aboriginal Being by Tony Swain, Cambridge University Press, 1993.

'Working with Indigenous Australians', Muswellbrook Shire Council, www.WorkingwithIndigenousAustralians.info

WHITE BUFFALO CALF WOMAN

Lame Deer, Seeker of Visions by Lame Deer and Richard Erdoes, Simon and Schuster, 1994.

'The Mythological Role of Gender Ideologies: A Crosscultural Sample of Traditional Cultures' by Richard Owens, *Nebraska Anthropologist,* vol. 17, 2002.

'Framework for Essential Understandings about American Indians', *Native Knowledge 360°*, Smithsonian National Museum of the American Indian, 2013.

A Native American Encyclopedia: History, Culture, and Peoples by Barry M. Pritzker, Oxford University Press, 2000.

Power of the Talking Stick: Indigenous Politics and the World Ecological Crisis by Sharon J. Ridgeway and Peter J. Jacques, Routledge, 2014.

'Native American History' by Elizabeth Prine Pauls, *Britannica Online*, 2008.

'Plains Indians' by Elizabeth Prine Pauls, *Britannica Online*, 2008.

Native American Mythology A to Z by Patricia Ann Lynch and Jeremy Roberts, Chelsea House, 2010.

Spider Woman's Web: Traditional Native American Tales About Women's Power by Susan Hazen-Hammond, Berkeley, 1999.

'The Lakota White Buffalo Calf Woman Narrative: A Cross-Literary Analysis' by (Tina) Theresa Hannah-Munns, Fourth Annual Research in Religious Studies Conference, University of Lethbridge, 2005.

The Legend of White Buffalo Calf Woman by Paul Goble, National Geographic, 1998.

'Lakota Culture', Akta Lakota Museum and Cultural Center, aktalakota.stjo.org.

'Important Message from Keeper of Sacred White

Buffalo Calf Pipe' by Chief Arvol Looking Horse, *Indian Country Today*, 2017.

'Respect' by Robin S. Dillon, *Stanford Encyclopedia of Philosophy*, 2018.

Teaching American Indian History: A Native American Voice by Donald A. Grinde Jr, *Perspectives on History*, American Historical Association, 1994.

'White Buffalo Calf Woman' told by John Lame Deer, National Museum of the American Indian, 1967.

'Towards a New Image of American Indian Women: The Renewing Power of the Feminine' by Marie Annette Jaimes, *Journal of American Indian Education*, vol. 22, 1982.

'Legend of the Teton Sioux Medicine Pipe' by George A. Dorsey, *Journal of American Folklore*, vol. 19, 1906.

Native American Myths and Legends edited by Jon E. Lewis, Constable and Robinson, 2013.

Native American Storytelling: A Reader of Myths and Legends, edited by Karl Kroeber, Blackwell, 2004.

Mythology of the American Nations by David M. Jones and Brian L. Molyneaux, Anness, 2001.

'Native American Foods: History, Culture and Influence on Modern Diets' by Sunmin Park, Nobuko Hongu and James W. Daily III, *Journal of Ethnic Foods*, vol. 3, issue 3, September 2016.

Reclaiming Native Truth: Changing the Narrative about Native Americans: A Guide for Allies by Echo Hawk Consulting and the First Nations Development Institute, 2018.

Acknowledgements

Our deepest thanks go to everyone at Faber who worked on this book, and our previous book *What Would Boudicca Do?*, with us: Laura, Louisa, Lizzie, Lauren, Niriksha, Camille, Emma, Camilla, Hattie, Hannah, Ella, Pedro, Donna, Paddy, Dave, Kate, Sam, Ian, Ruth, Alex and Stephen. We are also very grateful to Sara Adams and, of course and as ever, Oliver, Iris, Lola and Jeanie Bebb and Jack, Joseph, Barney and Leo Murphy.

Special extra thanks go to our teachers, friends and colleagues who inspired us when we were writing this book, and to everyone who came to see us at an event or contacted us or posted a nice review or sent a happy tweet or email to us about *Boudicca*. We hope you like this one too.